Airing Out Your Vagina

Being a Real Woman in an Unreal World

Written by:
Allie Trimble-Lozano

Table of Contents

Introduction

"Fuck this shit!" This is what I said to myself after the gazillionth time that I allowed someone to step over my boundaries. Mind you, they were invisible to them because I never learned that it is okay to set boundaries or to say no or to say fuck off to someone when they continuously disrespect you or try to take advantage of you. That is until I embarked on this journey of self-discovery that came with writing this book.

Sharing myself so openly with the world makes me feel incredibly vulnerable. So vulnerable, in fact, that I recently said to my counselor that I don't think the word vulnerable is sufficient to describe just how much of me I share in this book. The raw, unfiltered, unmasked, just plain to the core Allie. Baring it all, so to speak, is a scary idea to come to terms with. Then there's the concept of balancing speaking my truth and the impact that it could have on others. My intention here is to stand in my truth, in my power, and honor myself by doing so. Not to cast blame, shame, or

1

judge anyone else for where they are in their healing journey. I was really struggling with this concept on what to share and what not to share regarding the aspects of my story that overlap with that of others. I was listening to an episode of Mel Robbin's podcast where she was telling someone afraid of upsetting people in her life by sharing, to remember that she is telling her story. That this is HER experience and anyone and everyone in her life played a role in what that experience has been. I will say anyone who knows me knows that I am transparent to a fault. A straight shooter. A tell it like it is kinda gal. I'm working hard to live my life unapologetically in this phase and took this leap of faith because, at the risk of everything else, what I cannot allow is for me to find myself sitting on a porch 30 years from now, regretting not having taken a chance on myself.

I consider myself a pretty down-to-earth Texan (born in New Mexico or Mexican, as AJ used to think and call me) gal with a wicked sense of humor and the resilience of a cockroach. I'm that friend who makes it through life by sharing hilarious memes and witticisms that are usually loaded with a touch of wisdom and universal truths and heavy on sarcasm. Anyone who knows me is familiar with my witticisms, and that's what I've decided to base this book on. I see so many adult relationships and friendships being based on sharing memes these days. We're all just trying to survive, lifting each other up by sending hilarious memes back and forth. All the lessons I've learned are portrayed through stories and memes that I hope you'll be able to relate to throughout this book. Stories that will sometimes have you laughing out loud one moment and perhaps identifying with my truths so much that you'll be crying the next.

If you've picked up this book hoping for a tale of a damsel in distress, you might be somewhat disappointed. Not because I haven't had my fair share of distressing moments but because I've learned to transform them into damsel-*in-this-dress* moments. Yes, life has thrown a whole lemon tree's worth of lemons at me, but I picked those suckers up and made the best damn margaritas this side of the mighty Rio Grande. Perhaps I should've started the book with the line from the famous Marty Robbins song, "Down in the West Texas town of El Paso" as opposed to "fuck this shit," but I only get to write the first sentence of my first book once, and that just has a better ring to it!

At some point in your life, you may find yourself at a place where you've had enough. You've had enough of making yourself smaller and quieter so others may feel more comfortable. You may be tired of jumping through hoops just so you can exist as a woman, freely and in all her glory. Tired of being told what to do, when, and how to do it by people who have no inkling of what it means to carry the world's future in your uterus. Perhaps you'll reach the point where you're tired of playing small. Of doubting yourself, your worth, innate beauty, intelligence, capabilities, rights, and admirable inner strength.

If this is you, then welcome!

From the busy streets of El Paso, Texas, to the sterile corridors of hospitals, my journey has been a roller coaster ride. And trust me, it has had its ups, downs, and those in-between moments where you're not sure whether you're about to pull off something incredible or fall ass over tits face-first into the mud.

The life of a CEO is often glamorized with images of power suits, brisk walks, and sharp, commanding voices. But let me tell you, as the female CEO of three hospitals, some days, it takes all I can muster to make trivial decisions around whether I should wear the navy blue or black heels. And then there's the time I walked up to work wearing two entirely different shoes! However, this book isn't about fashion choices. It's about choices that fashion a life.

Have you ever felt like you're expected to do it all and do it well?

Look pretty, but not too pretty because then you're inviting unwanted attention. Work hard, but not too hard, because you must also take care of the kids. Dress up, but not too provocatively, because that'll land you in trouble when men can't control themselves, and other women will hate you for looking better than they do. Because you asked for it, right? Be assertive but never challenge a man or come across as a bitch to an insecure woman. Be friendly, but not too friendly. Don't be a slut. Be a good mother, but don't talk about your kids too much. Be extraordinary, but do it on the down low. Be a provider, but don't achieve too much success, as it'll bruise your partner's ego. Do as you're told, and be grateful for every opportunity.

Fuck that, I say. I am woman, hear me roar, and all that jazz.

I wouldn't particularly consider myself a feminist, but man, do all these double standards grind my gears.

Women are often expected to do it all and do it with a smile. Just because we can do it alone doesn't mean we should have to.

This book is all about what it means to be a woman in a world where we are constantly underestimated, taken advantage of, and robbed of our human rights. Please don't get me wrong; I'm not out to slander men as a species entirely. Because, let's face it, they are a different species to us women. We all learned years ago that men are from Mars and women are from Venus. This is all about not allowing anyone to do anything to you that you don't want or approve of. Not allowing anyone, regardless of sex, race, age, religion, nationality, or place in your world to have any say in who you are and how you choose to live your life.

So join me on this journey as I share my life with you. As a daughter. As a qualified nurse. As an MBA holder. As a CEO. As a divorcee. As a single mother. As a fish out of the online dating app water. As a woman trying to navigate this crazy world.

If I can make one woman laugh, cry, or feel a little less bat-shit crazy about what's going on in her head, then this will all be worth it.

Buckle up, buttercup! You're in for a rollercoaster of a ride!

Chapter 1

Big Girl Panties & Lipstick

Stephanie, my hospital pharmacist, walks into my office. I have my mom on the phone, who's upset because her prescription for her medication to treat her depression isn't covered by insurance, complaining about how expensive the medications are; I have my boy's school on my office phone because he's in the nurse's room and his dad who has him this week isn't answering his phone; MD Anderson Cancer Treatment Center is messaging me because someone needs to sign for my father's prescription but no one is home; my 5th boss in seven years is calling me on Teams wanting to discuss the fact that the VP of the people experience team reached out to him because I didn't return a phone call I never actually received; and we're busy handling a pharmacy audit issue, which is why Stephanie stopped by in the first place.

But it's okay; I am a woman. I can do everything. I can be a single mom, a CEO of three hospitals, a provider, a sister, a daughter, a caretaker, a shoulder to cry on, a boss lady, an employee, and a partner, and, and and…

Stephanie stands at the door, leaning against the door frame, and asks, "*How do you do it all?*" My answer? "*Coffee and alcohol, sister.*" The thing is, as the years go by, the gap between when I consume coffee and when I switch over to alcohol seems to be shrinking rapidly. They both provide sanity in a cup/glass/bottle. Liquid strength and liquid courage, depending on what's necessary, hence the time between the two getting closer and closer together! Whatever is needed to make it through another day, right? (Note: I'm not promoting addiction. I'm promoting sanity, okay, Karen?)

The truth is that when you start bearing the weight of a significant title, you can't just fake it till you make it. You have to just do it! You have to face it until you make it. Every day! Not like the firing squad death penalty where the quote came from, but more like the Nike version where you put on the uniform and show up as your best self every damn day until it's *mission accomplished.* (Infamous serial killer Gary Gilmore's last words on death row, as he stood in front of a firing squad, were, "*Let's do this.*" This is reportedly the source of inspiration for Nike's famous tagline that reads, "*Just do it.*")[1]

To be perfectly honest, sometimes, when people ask me how I do it, I want to reply by saying that I wasn't given a choice. Sometimes, we have no choice but to be the glue that holds it all together. Because if I don't, who will? It's a nice idea to think that my world would be fine if I chose not to do it all. That someone else would step up and alternate the gift and the opportunity to take my dad to all his cancer treatment visits in Houston. That someone else will fight the totally unrealistic budget being shoved down from the home office. That someone else will get in touch with a roofer to come to repair the roof leak that caused the puddle that caused my broken butt when I slipped and fell in it this morning. Someone else will make arrangements and figure out how to get my son to and from his shortened school day while I run my board meeting. That maybe, just maybe, someone else would figure out how to be everything for everyone while I come up for air for just a moment. However, I can say with some confidence that this would not be the case.

Sometimes, you just don't have a choice, especially as a woman.

We've been taught all our lives that we need to be the caretakers. And I do not doubt that you're probably saying, *"Yeah, but that's your choice,"* aren't you, Karen? Okay, so practice your free will and stop doing everything you've been doing for everyone around you for your entire adult life. See how happy your little world remains and for how long? Stop feeding your children and your husband/wife. Stop working and earning an income. Stop taking your dad to Houston every month to get the all-important cancer treatment he needs because no one else can do it. Stop advocating for your child at school because he has some special needs that many teachers just don't care to understand. Stop all of it, and let's see how happy you are with *choosing* not to take on all the things that have been put on your plate. Some of us don't have the luxury of choice, and it's ignorant to think that everyone does.

I love the idea of fostering positivity. I really do. I'm all for it. However, sometimes, life is not all sunshine and butterflies. Sometimes, instead of lemons, life throws darts at you, and it's just not fun anymore. It hurts.

Don't get me wrong. Life truly is a gift, and I greatly appreciate the fact that I get to live this life and have the experience of being a human on Earth. The odds of you or I being here are astounding. Apparently, the odds of you being here, living this life you're living right now, are one in four hundred trillion! So, obviously, we're meant to be here. However, that doesn't mean that we need to smile through *all the shit all the time*, pretending like it doesn't stink. The flip side is that if you sit in shit for long enough, it stops smelling. You need to get out of there before that happens, or you're liable to sit in it forever.

Sometimes I sit back and look at my life, and I think, *"Man, isn't this delightful?"* Then there are the days when it's more of a *"What the actual fuck is going on?"* scenario. I don't know about you, but I feel like I'm having more and more WTF days as we progress through this twenty-first century.

Even so, I absolutely love my life in so many aspects, and I feel grateful for so many blessings on a daily basis. I have an amazing job and a gorgeous and talented boy who keeps me on my toes and whom I love to death. He is the why to the question, *"What is my purpose on Earth?"*

Yes. Every day is a gift. But some days are underwear. And that's okay.

Some days are just fucked, and no amount of lemonade is going to unfuck it. Hence the margaritas for a little liquid optimism! Do you know what you should do then? Go home, get back into bed, and try again tomorrow.

I don't have that kind of liberty, and I'm guessing you don't either. No. We have bills to pay, children to keep alive, partners to accommodate, health that needs maintaining, sanity that needs keeping, etc.

It's not all doom and gloom, though. Life is a series of ebbs and flows, and we're just along for the ride.

I know better days are coming, but when? Can I get an ETA, please? It would be nice to know that when you've had a shitty day, tomorrow is going to be a better one, right? Something to look forward to. Something to take the weight off.

I've said on more than one occasion that if I have to pull up my big girl panties one more time, the elastic is gonna snap, and I'm going to show more of my ass than anyone ever wanted to see. I might be a CEO, but I definitely don't have the financial means to pay for all of El Paso's therapy.

I certainly don't have it all figured out, and I've had to learn that that's okay. It's okay not always to be smiling. It's okay to struggle. It's okay to want to punch someone in the face sometimes (emphasis on "*want*"). It's okay to want to day-drink sometimes. (To all my colleagues reading this, I don't). It's okay not to be okay.

Sometimes, you're so busy trying to keep all the balls in the air that you don't even realize that you might not be entirely okay. That is until you're sitting in a meeting and looking down at your feet just to realize you're wearing *TWO DIFFERENT SHOES*! So that happened. I must've been in a rush to get to work on this day and just grabbed a pair of shoes off my shoe rack. They were both cream-colored, but what makes it hilarious is that one had a leopard print stiletto-style heel and the other a plain block-type wedged heel. Needless to say, I burst out laughing the moment I realized what I'd done and had to take a picture, of course. It's also the moment I thought, "*Maybe we need a break.*" My big girl panties were definitely not big enough that day.

Life is not a linear experience. You'll have good days, bad days, overwhelming days, I got this days, I'm too tired days, awesome days, I can't go on days, but every day you'll still show up. Today, you might be on top of the world, and tomorrow, you're lying with your face in the dirt. That's life. She can be a real bitch sometimes. Sometimes, you'll fail and fall down. But then you get back up again. You learn from your mistakes and try to do it better next time. This is how we grow.

I love the analogy of how a lump of coal must be put under tremendous pressure to form into a diamond. Hardship sucks. I know. But it is what gives life meaning. If we can reframe how we see the challenges given to us, it becomes more bearable. When you start choosing to view supposed failures as opportunities to learn and grow from, you embrace the lessons. This is the difference between those who realize their dreams and live in line with their highest purpose versus those who just keep dreaming. It's the difference between the "*todays*" and the "*somedays*." There's this saying I love that goes: "*You get to choose. It's either one day or day one.*"

No matter how you feel, you've got to GET UP, DRESS UP, and SHOW UP.

Yes, you of course need to look after yourself and take time off when you need it. I'm all for that, for sure. However, I do feel like all the hype around fostering positivity on social media can turn into toxic positivity—quite the oxymoron, I know. What I mean by toxic positivity is that you can think all the positive thoughts you want when you're feeling down in the dumps, when you're feeling depressed, or even suicidal. I can guarantee you that all those positive thoughts will do exactly jack shit to get you out of that hole, if they aren't combined with action.

So many people believe that self-care exclusively involves spa days, manicures, or some form of indulgence. When true self-care, in fact, entails doing the things you don't feel like doing but need to do to take care of yourself, like making your bed, showering, eating healthy, hitting the gym, seeing your therapist, setting and maintaining boundaries, squeezing in your alone time etc. That's how you climb out of the hole when you've fallen in yet again.

You fall into the hole, take a breather, do what you need to do to take care of yourself while you're down in that hole, and then slowly climb back out again. You fall again, you get up again, you carry on. You work hard, you fail, you fall, you learn, you get back up–rinse, wash, repeat.

The best we can aim for is to strike a balance between grit and grace.

I consider myself a pretty gritty person. I've been around the block a few times. However, there are still moments that cause me to be taken aback. My problem, sometimes, is that words seem to exit my mouth before having the opportunity to pass through my brain. Filter, you say? But where's the fun in that?

Like when I had the audacity to speak up in a particularly important meeting attended by top corporate management of the different facilities I managed at the time. I'm a numbers girl. I like data because data never lies. On this particular day, I made a suggestion based on data that concerned pediatric care.

Well! As I exited the boardroom, a six-foot-something figure of a man, one of the main company executives, cornered me and said, *"Before you go nut-knocking in here again, talk to me first!"* I was taken aback, mainly because I didn't know what the term *"nut-knocking"* meant. I could infer from context, of course. However, my mouth got the jump on my brain, and before I could stop myself, I said: *"Sir, I'm not sure what "nut-knocking" is, so I'll have to look that up later. I presume your intended accusation was that I was ball-busting in a room full of male executives, but the truth of the matter is, sir, that the data presented absolutely supports the business plan case."*

Well, let's just say that some men's egos are too fragile to handle any competition, especially from a woman and especially in the business world. Luckily, this particular individual and I ended our professional tenure together with a great deal of respect for one another. I realized I was the first vocal outsider to be hired into a company of longstanding insiders, and he realized that my intention was only ever to help make his company perform even better.

It's not just men's egos, though. Another incident that comes to mind is when I made a suggestion to a senior nurse, and her response to me was: *"Listen here, missy, I've been a nurse for thirty-four years!"* Before I knew it, I responded, "*Oh wow, you've been a nurse longer than I've been alive!"* This was a while back, and there's not enough money in the world that could make me want to go back from my 40s!

The fact of the matter is that the best idea should win. Too long have men spoken over and dismissed the ideas of women in boardrooms because they, unfortunately, fall victim to their egos.

Women must also start sticking together and standing up for one another. Just because another woman in a senior position tries to communicate a suggestion doesn't mean she's trying to insinuate that you don't know what you're doing. Egos on both sides should be put aside.

Like I said. The best idea should always win. Not tenure with a list of initials. Have you ever worked for someone who feels the need to remind you constantly of their title in the company? Not usually a sign of a good leader, or a competent one honestly.

I've long learned that I need to stand up for myself in my personal life and in business. For most of my life, I've longed for someone to say, *"I've got you, Allie."* I realized relatively recently that I'm it. I have to catch myself and have my own back. The realization that I can say *"I got you, Allie"* to myself has been incredibly empowering. I still yearn for someone who might someday enter my life, but in the meantime, I've got myself.

Life isn't easy. I don't think a single human being on this planet would say otherwise. I don't think it was ever meant to be easy. Anything that's worth having always comes with some struggle or obstacle attached to it. It's what makes it so worth it. It's what makes it so rewarding.

I'm happy as long as I can get through it with a bit of grace.

Chapter 2

Tits Up

Tits up!

Before this book, I never realized that this saying has different meanings in different parts of the world and to different people. In this age, we have become a global village, and the writer who helped me in the journey of writing this book is from a different part of the world. As we're working on this chapter, she tells me that the term "tits up" has a different meaning where she comes from compared to mine.

To me, the phrase "*tits up*" has always had the same positive connotation as "sun's out, buns out," or something similar. To me, the phrase means that when the going gets tough, you need to puff out your chest and get your "tits up." I fell further in love with this saying when I watched "The Marvelous Mrs. Maisel." Suzie, her agent, would tell Midge "*Tits up*" right before she took the stage, essentially saying "you've got this".

Where my book coach comes from, the phrase means that something is broken. When a situation has gone to shit, you say, *"Everything's gone tits up."*

She checked where it originally came from, and it is believed that it comes from when airplanes' altitude indicators would "turn upside down when faulty and display an inverted 'W' resembling a pair of breasts."[2]

Now you know.

This chapter is about facing fear with courage, getting your tits up, and facing whatever comes your way when the proverbial shit hits the fan. (Just remember to keep your mouth closed.)

I certainly know that I have felt paralyzed by fear more times than I care to admit. Sometimes, that fear would grip me to the point where I'd get some boob sweat going. I know you girls know what I'm talking about. What I've always wondered though is why it is called "boob sweat" and not *"humidititties?"*

Like the time I dared to take on the tenor sax solo in junior high jazz band and having to deal with this all-encompassing fear of screwing it up. Especially with being the daughter of a renowned professional musician. Then there's the time I decided to apply for the market CEO job, where I now run three different hospitals! I never thought I'd actually get it. Lions, tigers, and jumping from great heights, bring it on! But judgment and criticism from others?! That's always been my worst fear. The fear of not being "good enough." The same goes for writing this book and putting myself "out there." It scares the bejesus out of me.

Then, I remind myself that Courage is not the absence of fear. It's feeling afraid and doing it anyway.

I read somewhere once that the word FEAR can mean one of two things. It can either mean to Fear Everything And Run or Face Everything And

Rise. Which one do you choose on a daily basis? With the emphasis on *choose*.

Harvard Medical School psychologist Susan David famously said in one of her TED Talks, "*Discomfort is the cost of admission to a meaningful life*." Her talks and coaching are all about emotional agility and how "tough emotions are part of our contract with life." I don't remember signing a contract, but whatever.

Another of my favorite quotes is by Margaret Shepard: "*Sometimes, your only available mode of transportation is a leap of faith*." Thank you for sharing this one with me Ames…it has been life changing!

The experience of fear as an emotion can be so overwhelmingly debilitating that it keeps us from taking action when needed. It can make us lose faith in others, but especially in ourselves. Some call it the "inner critic," but I choose to call it "*the asshole that lives in my mind*." It's that voice that tells you that you cannot do it. That you're not good enough. That you're not worthy. That you're not capable. You'll embarrass yourself. You know, like a typical asshole would. Fuck that guy!

Instead of listening to that asshole, imagine what might happen if you choose to focus on the fact that you don't need anyone's permission to do whatever the fuck you want! Unless you're planning to be an asshole of some sort, then I'd say you'd need to get some help. Otherwise, you can do absolutely anything you set your mind to.

Yes, some have more resources than others. Some people are born into poverty, whereas others are born holding a silver spoon. Some are born with disabilities, whereas others are born perfectly able-bodied. But you know what? I've seen people without limbs living their best lives as motivational speakers and people born into war-torn countries taking on governments by themselves on an international stage. So what's your excuse? I'm scared? I think not!

Strength and courage aren't necessarily something we're inherently born with. It's something you need to cultivate through choice and practice on a regular basis.

You need to realize that while you sit in fear, paralyzed by your own self-doubt, there are people who are intimidated by your potential.

If you're reading this book, you have survived 100% of the hardships you've faced in your life to date. Perhaps you should give yourself more credit. You're stronger than you think you are. You don't have to prove your worth. You were born worthy.

You simply have to choose whether you want to take up the challenge laid at your feet or not. Or will you allow fear to dictate the level of your life's achievements and happiness? I personally do not think that one should so easily give your own power away. I'm not saying it's easy. None of this is easy! Simple yes; easy hell no!

I went a long time in my life without really paying attention to the thoughts that pop in and out of my head on a daily basis. We think thousands of thoughts every single day and process an inordinate amount of information in our environments. Even so, the amount our brains process is only a fraction of what goes on. The human body sends eleven million bits per second of information to the brain for processing. Your conscious mind only focuses on a tiny amount of information available in your immediate environment. Imagine if it focused on every single tiny detail of what you take in through your senses at any given moment. It would be a shit show. Instead, we are only aware of the necessary information.

Have you ever taken a moment to turn your awareness to your thoughts? Have you ever tried to understand the underlying root of your thoughts or beliefs? Where does it come from? Why is it there? And perhaps the most important question of all is, does it serve you? Is it helpful?

Because I can assure you the asshole in your brain that keeps telling you that you're not pretty enough or smart enough or worthy enough doesn't serve your highest purpose. In fact, I'd bet my hard-earned money on it.

They call it mindfulness. Before I really understood what mindfulness meant, I'd imagine Elizabeth Gilbert, who wrote "Eat, Pray, Love" on her meditation quest, talking to Ketut, who told her to smile from her liver. With that caffeine/alcohol window of mine shrinking by the day, my liver might be smiling way too much these days.

I have since learned that mindfulness is just being able to turn your attention to what's going on right here, in and outside of you. It's a proven practice to treat all sorts of ailments and issues in humans, ranging from anxiety to depression, stress, chronic overthinking, etc. It is also the ability to tune into what's going on upstairs in your mind.

I personally think that the majority of us live our lives fairly unconsciously. A great example of this is when we arrive home and have zero recollection of the drive and how we got there. We are pulling in the driveway and literally can't remember a thing from the drive. If I had to ask you how often you pay attention to the little stuff in your environment or how often you choose to turn your attention to what's going on inside your mind when you're feeling emotionally triggered, what would your answer be?

The way you talk to yourself and the thoughts and beliefs you allow yourself to focus on will predict just about everything in your life. What is going on on the inside predicts what you'll experience on the outside. I know, I'm sounding like I've maybe gotten into some edibles. Seriously though. I feel like the older I get, the more I realize that the true meaning in life cannot be found in material belongings. We must turn inward and have the courage to ask the hard questions.

- Why do I struggle with the things I struggle with? Where does it come from?

- Why do I react to certain triggers the way I do?

- What are my triggers and why?

- Why don't I feel worthy?

- How often do I make time for myself?

- How often do I allow others to walk over me?

- How often do I say yes to others but no to myself, and why?

- Why do I fear going for the biggest, boldest dream in my head?

- Why do I allow the opinions of others to dictate my inner state and actions?

Tough questions, I know. Again, simple…NOT EASY!

You see, school doesn't equip us to be successful in life. It doesn't teach us how to look after ourselves or our personal wellbeing. The schooling system we've all gone through was designed for an age we've long surpassed. What they should be teaching our children is:

- How to look after your own mental health.

- How to invest your money.

- How to be an entrepreneur.

- How to make money in the digital age.

- How to regulate your emotions.

- How to garner a growth mindset in life.

- How to be a decent human being.

Granted, parents should, of course, also be teaching their children these things. But let's face it, they spend more time at school than they do with us as working parents. This issue has been magnified and compounded by the mass exodus of qualified and quality educators that left the field during and following the pandemic. I have a lot of educators in my family and friend circle who give it everything they've got, but sadly often that isn't the case anymore. It's just a means to a paycheck to many. I was so disheartened one day this last school year when I picked AJ up from school. He was supposed to have been in tutoring but was sitting outside sweaty and hot. When I inquired as to why he wasn't in tutoring, admittedly assuming the worst of him, he shared that his English teacher had said she was no longer offering tutoring or any form of before or afterschool support because she wasn't paid overtime for it and was tired of complaining about it. This is not to say that is everyone, as another of his teachers that same year bent over backwards to support his success in her class.

I wish someone had taught me how to pay attention to my inner thoughts and how not to allow the asshole in my brain to bully me into not believing in myself when I was in school.

Think about it. You get this life you're living here and now, only ONCE! ONE SHOT! Only one. Even if you believe in reincarnation, you still only get THIS life once. And will you allow fear or other people's opinions to keep you from living boldly?

NO! Get rid of that asshole. Do whatever it is you need to do to throw him out. Serve him an eviction notice in the form of therapy, self-help courses, or whatever it is you need, and kick his ass out.

Don't you dare waste this precious opportunity you've been given! Do you really want to look back ten, twenty, thirty years from now and be filled with regrets because you didn't take that chance or didn't go after what you really wanted? Will it have been worth it...listening to the asshole in your brain instead of following your dreams?

Get ready for some bumper sticker talk: You miss 100% of the shots you don't take. You'll never have it if you don't go after what you want. If you don't ask, the answer will always be no. If you don't take the risk of stepping forward, you'll just stay in the same spot.

And then we haven't even touched on imposter syndrome yet. That's another asshole a lot of us have to deal with. I sometimes wonder if people who suffer from narcissistic personality disorder ever experience imposter syndrome. I doubt it. I'm not saying you should become a narcissist, though. This world has way too many of them in it already.

It's just another thing that doesn't really help you or serve you in any meaningful way.

As a child, I was always taught never to "toot my own horn." And although it is the kind of thing I also try to instill in my own child, I do think we need to revise this rule.

Not to mean that we should all become social-media-flaunting jackasses. There are plenty of those, too. I'm trying to say that society needs to unlearn this idea that you're not allowed to be proud of yourself or rather to show that you're proud of yourself. I think we've kinda missed the boat a bit on this one, and I genuinely believe it's one of the main reasons why so few of us know how to love and accept ourselves. You should be able to flaunt your achievements proudly. You've worked hard for those and deserve recognition. Most of us have been taught to keep it all to ourselves. Be humble. Don't brag. Sure, don't be an ass about it, but also, be unashamedly awesome. It's a bit like we've been taught to *Strive to be your best self and achieve all the things you want, but don't talk about it.*

Imagine if we changed that attitude and actually started cheering each other on. Imagine if you changed your attitude and started cheering *yourself* on!

Self-doubt = Asshole.
Imposter syndrome = Asshole.
Fear = Asshole.
Fuck that unholy trinity.

Imposter syndrome can be a particularly resilient asshole in my life. Especially as a woman working at the executive level in a (still) male-dominated industry at the top. Kinda mind-blowing to think that in a heavily female-dominated field such as healthcare, the top echelon is still heavily male-dominated. I've often had to catch myself when my thoughts of self-doubt creep in during boardroom meetings.

You know, questions like: "Who am I to make these suggestions?" or "Who am I to write a book?" or "Why would anyone take me seriously?"

It took me a long time to learn that the issue doesn't lie with others taking you seriously. The real issue is whether you take yourself seriously. Because when you are secure within yourself, your knowledge, your abilities, and your experience, what others may think of you becomes a non-issue. A lioness doesn't concern herself with the opinion of a sheep. You are a strong and powerful lioness; you need not fear anything.

Do you know why we have vaginas and not a penis and testicles as our male counterparts? It's because our balls have always been too big to fit down there, so God put them on our chest. "Chesticles," if you will. Now, when I sit at the boardroom table, I think, "I'm a lioness with balls bigger than any of yours. Try and test me. That'll be fun."

It's time that we stop fixating on everything that could go wrong and get excited about all the things that could go right!

One of my favorite quotes ever comes from S.L. Heston and reads, "*I was lying flat on my back in the middle of a place called rock bottom, and through the tears I saw it, one small ray of light, and beyond the screams of why I heard it, a faint whisper of hope. I will forever be searching for a reason to believe because, you see, falling down has always been my forte, but staying down will never be my style. I will rise.*"

Staying down has never, and will never be my style. I will always rise again! I talk a lot about music and its profound impact on my life. That said, I couldn't write "I will rise" and not advise everyone reading this to pause here and listen to "Rise Up" by Andra Day. It's a powerful one and a mantra in its own right. And while you're at it, read one of my all-time favorite poems. "Still I Rise" by the great Dr. Maya Angelou.

Now, take THAT asshole in my brain!

Chapter 3

I'm Fine. It's Fine. Everything is Fine.

I love being a strong, independent woman. I really do! However, sometimes I wish I could just let go and have someone catch me for a change.

Strong, independent women will always say, "I'm fine." I guess because we rarely have a choice. I'll be running on empty, barely holding it together, but when someone asks me how I'm doing, my answer is usually, "I'm fine." Because I have a family that depends on me, I have a boy who needs his momma, and although I'm working on fostering a healthy co-parenting environment, it can be quite tricky.

Then there's my dad. My brilliant musician of a father who just wants everyone to get along. He's getting on and sadly dealing with terminal cancer. Being the only one in the family who's capable and willing, I fly with him to Houston monthly for him to receive the treatment he needs, over and above my job, while being a single mom. I do it because I love my father dearly and want him to receive the treatment he needs.

On our trips back and forth between Houston and El Paso, we often have these more profound, meaningful talks. I'm exceptionally grateful for this time with him, mostly because I never had that with my dad until he got sick. However, I get a little sad whenever he expresses that he's not worried about me because he knows I'm strong and that I'll figure it out. That he instead worries about my mom and my brother. Some things don't ever change.

I get sad because he doesn't quite seem to understand when I tell him I'm not this way because I chose to be. I'm this way because I had to be. People perceive me as strong and "together" because I *must* be. Not just for myself but primarily for others. The people who depend on me. My team at the hospitals. My son. My mom. My dad. My brother. I'm the fixer. The executor. The problem solver. And I always have been. Because if I don't do it, who will?

This became even more glaringly clear recently when Dad stated after our most recent trip that my brother would like to try to start going on some of these trips to Houston with him. Don't get me wrong; I wouldn't trade the talks and the alone time we've had this last year-and-a-half for anything, but it's been close to 30 trips. When he shared this, I said it would be wonderful if my brother and I could start to alternate. It was a gut-punch when my dad responded that he'd give the dates for the next trip to my brother, and if he could rearrange his work schedule to take him, he'd go with him, and if my brother wasn't able to adjust his schedule, he'd have me go. I just stood there, kinda dumbfounded. My brother is unmarried, has no children, and has an essentially virtual job unless he's presenting at a conference. Nevertheless, if he can adjust his schedule, he'll go, but if he can't, the hospital CEO and single mother will need to adjust hers so she can go. I don't think for one moment that my dad had ill intent in saying what he said, but it spoke volumes to me about the way I've always felt, perhaps not being all in my head after all.

People who need to "fix" others generally develop this need out of wanting to be seen and accepted by others. If you are always there for others and if you are always helping others, maybe they'll see you and love you. Maybe they'll provide you with the nurturing you never received as a child. I needed and desired the same attention and support that my brother received, but I didn't require or demand it the same way he did. In many ways, I raised myself while they were busy raising him. I don't think I realized until more recently that this behavior is still very prevalent in the family dynamic. What he wants, he gets because it's not worth the argument. Or because, "*Well, you know how he is.*" Or, "*That's just him.*"

My parents did their best, and I adore them both; however, my father is the proverbial pacifist and creative. He was always busy with his music and extra playing jobs to help support our family. Then, if we're ripping off the Band-Aids and being honest, he had a love of golf and hobbies my mom didn't have the luxury of having. That often left mom alone to deal with two kids and homework, keeping a house in order, etc. Mom has struggled with severe ADHD and debilitating depression most of her life, and both my parents have always had their hands full with my brother. The focus has always mainly been on accommodating him and his needs in an effort to keep the peace. Unfortunately, that enablement and pacification kept the peace for him at the expense of those who loved him. Family first and keeping the peace led to the constant swallowing of my feelings and my needs, which has had quite an impact on my personal well-being, both physical and emotional.

I have always done whatever I can to support the ones I love, at times to a fault: my dad and his cancer, my mom and her guilt, my brother and his challenges, work and the responsibilities that come with the title, and don't get me started on the attempted rescue of my ex from his failure to launch. Regarding Dad, like I said, I so cherish the time we get to spend together on his trips to get treatment. He is immensely grateful and voices it regularly, and I'm earnest in my response, which is that I wouldn't trade these times together for anything! He worries and says he never wanted to live long enough to become a burden, and I reassure him that he is FAR from a burden. He is my dad! This is alone time with just Dad and me, which I've never had. It breaks my heart to know it took a terminal cancer diagnosis, a wife in no physical or mental condition to do it, a brother who was initially unavailable, and a daughter who's a nurse with the expertise in this field for us to make that time. It's also immensely stressful as we never know what news we'll get back from a scan and how I'd then have to relay that to the rest of the family.

My mom and helping her get the treatment she needs for her debilitating depression and her belief that my brother is "her fault." And because my son has some similar struggles with ADHD and impulse control, she blames herself for that as well. I've explained to my mom that we all have challenges but are ultimately responsible for our behavior and how we treat others.

Then there's my brother and his career and relationship endeavors. I've always stood by and cheered him on. I remember how shocked I was at a comment he made several years ago about "now being tied" when he closed on a second rental property. I realized at that moment he'd lived his life in competition with me. That idea had never even occurred to me, but it explained so much. I've wanted nothing more than for him to be healthy and happy in his life. He's incredibly talented at what he does, and I'm proud of him for his achievements. However, I worry it will never be fulfilling to him. He always needs the next recognition. The next compliment or award. Seeking the next promotion or company that will value him and see his worth instead of seeking that within himself. Same goes for the women in his life, just never quite enough.

Making sure my team has everything they need to do their jobs well and thrive in the workplace and beyond. Being there for friends who are navigating difficulties in their own lives. I spent the better half of two decades trying to support my ex into success and happiness. Dealing with my own romantic relationships when I'm crazy enough to try again. Making sure my boy AJ is safe and looked after, providing whatever he needs with the ultimate goal of raising a good quality man.

Then, in those rare moments when I'm able to sit down and take a deep breath, I think to myself, "Who's got Allie's back?" Who's going to come pick me up if I fall? The answer to that question came to me not too long ago. I realized the answer to that question was no one. The ONLY person I can depend on to be there with and for me until the end is ME! *"I've got me."*

Which is why it's so important that we take the time to look after ourselves. You can control only two things in your life: the way you prepare for what might happen and how you respond to what happens to and inside of you. I think society teaches us that it's not okay to express difficulty. I know that, for the longest time, generations before me considered it taboo to speak about anything related to struggle, whether physical, financial, emotional, or mental. It's like they'd been programmed to view struggle as a weakness.

I've seen society slowly evolving and moving away from this frame of mind, which I'm really grateful for because it's a toxic belief system. It's a system that brought up generations of men who cannot deal with their own emotions because they were never allowed to express them. Some seek refuge at the bottom of a bottle or in a syringe. Others avoid it, diving into work or hobbies or other women. Then, they take it out on their children and their wives when these don't fix their deep need for love and acceptance. Some women become bitter, angry men haters. I choose to see each individual, male or female, and make a decision based solely on their behavior. I'm blessed in that my dad is extremely sensitive. Shows emotion freely. I can't tell you how many times we've stood in tears at events when they play the national anthem! He simply cannot have the difficult conversations sometimes required in any family. He's too much of a pacifist, and emotions simply overwhelm him. To hold the line and set boundaries and expectations is too hard for him. His escapes have always been his music and golf. As the years passed, that led to a great deal of time together for him and my brother and not so much for me and my mom. We somehow became the outsiders in our own family.

Women have been oppressed for centuries, having to fight for our right to exist basically. For our right to vote. For our right to study. For our right to work. I mean, how ridiculous is it that any human being has to fight for the right to do what they want to with their own God-given life? Because one of my favorite lines is, "You've got one hell of a set of chesticles" Sometime recently, I wondered to myself that if the size of men's penises were so easily and prominently displayed as our breasts, how would the world react? It's absurd.

It gets to me sometimes, as I'm sure it also does to you. I think it affects us all in different ways. That's when I remind myself that it's okay to lose my shit temporarily instead of trying to hold it all in and allow it to rot me from the inside out and become bitter and resentful. I allow myself to do whatever it is I need to do to let it all out. Cry in the shower, scream into a pillow, go to the garage, and stomp my feet like an animal (or a four-year-old). Single-player carpool karaoke at the top of my lungs! Love me some Pink!! Have you ever tried going to one of those rage rooms? You know, where you pay to fuck shit up with a baseball bat or whatever weapon fancies your need to rage against the machine. I think we all need a good half an hour in one of those once in a while just to let it all out. Because if you keep all that shit inside of you, you end up full of shit. Then, when the day comes and you explode, there'll be shit everywhere. It'll be a shitstorm! Nobody wants that.

We could all use a check-up from the neck up occasionally because most of us still don't know how to express ourselves or deal with our emotions honestly. We don't trust one another and, thereby, never learn how to be truly vulnerable. We think about it but are so concerned with how what we share might be perceived that we just keep it to ourselves. Depending on where it's occurring, of course. If I set a boundary and say, "I will no longer allow you to berate and disrespect me," then will I lose my whole friend group? My job? My whole family? Perhaps the lesson is that those who choose not to respect the boundaries you set do not deserve to be in your life. That you deserve better. You deserve people who choose to respect you, your needs, and your boundaries.

Sometimes, when you try to open yourself up, you choose the wrong person to be vulnerable with. They end up being a pathological narcissist who later uses it against you as a weapon to hurt you when the relationship goes in the pooper.

So now, when someone asks how you are, the answer is always "fine." Am I right?

Let me decipher it for you in case you haven't figured it out yet.

When I say I'm "fine," it actually means, "I don't want to talk about it" or "I don't want to talk to you about it."

When I say, "Living the dream," it actually means "I don't know what to say."

When I say, "I'm a little tired, but good," it means "kill me, kill me now."

When I say, "I'm hanging in there," it means "by a noose."

29

One of my favorites these days when things are really rough is "I'm looking down at the dirt, so there's that."

Social media has this way of making you think that everyone else's lives are amazing and you're the only asshole struggling. Which means there must be something inherently wrong with you, right? Wrong. Social media is a lie. Everyone is struggling one way or another. We just don't show it to the rest of the world.

Sweet 'ol Mimi, who owns Mimi's nail salon, told me recently that when I first started going there, she looked at me and thought, "*It must be nice to have it all. A great job, financially stable, attractive, funny, smart, etc.*" She only confessed this to me after well over a year of visiting her every other week to have my nails done. Only after a year has she learned the truth of the struggles I face on a daily basis, both in my work and personal life. She now sees me as a strong woman who has been dealt many low blows in her life but just keeps going. And just for added impact, Mimi doesn't know the half of it!

We're always quick to assume what's going on in someone else's life. We always think the grass is greener on the other side or that everyone else has it better or easier than us. The fact of the matter is that we all have our own shit to deal with. Some more than others, sure, but no one goes unscathed in this life or on this planet. Everyone has scars that they carry but never speak of.

If we could only learn to treat each other with just an ounce more grace, imagine how that might change our world. I see so many thousands of trolls who try to break others down with their comments on social media all day long. What a sad existence if that's all you have to contribute to society. It is a choice that someone makes, day in and day out. Imagine what pain and insecurity individuals must carry within themselves to want to hurt someone else for the sheer fun of it. It's diabolical.

This is perhaps one of the main reasons why so many people don't speak up when they need help. I believe so many of us feel that we're a burden to others when we reach out for help. Because this one has bigger issues than you, and that one is currently dealing with their own stuff.

I'd bet anything, though, that you'd want your friend or loved one to feel that they could come to you with their problems instead of keeping it inside to the point where they may see no other way out than the ultimate way out, which is the pandemic of suicide we're currently seeing happening in the world. Did you know that post the COVID-19 pandemic, somewhere in the world, someone dies by suicide every 40 seconds? EVERY 40 SECONDS!! Let that sink in. A life. A person. Gone. Forever. EVERY FORTY SECONDS!

I remember back in nursing school when the stress would run especially high, I'd say the only thing in life that you HAVE to do is breathe. Everything else is optional. You can live without food and water for a day. You can live without social media, well, forever. You can live without all things for an hour. But breathing? You can go for maybe 3 minutes if you have a good set of lungs. As long as we're breathing, we still have the opportunity to choose change. In the words of the great Mahatma Gandhi, "*If you want to change the world, start with yourself.*"

This section has quite a bit of anxiety attached to it, so on the point of breathing, here's a quick breathing exercise for you to try whenever you're feeling anxious or just out of sorts. This is something I do often, and AJ has started using it in moments of anxiety or when he feels overwhelmed at school.

It's called the 4-7-8 breathing technique. It is a type of mindfulness exercise, and the point of the exercise is to breathe out for longer than you breathe in. This activates your parasympathetic nervous system, which is the part of your nervous system that tells your body to chill out.

Here's how you do it: you start by breathing in through your nose for 4 seconds, then you hold your breath at the top for 7 seconds, and slowly breathe out for 8 seconds. You can then repeat this four or five times. Or a few minutes even, if that works better for you. You might find it difficult to breathe out for 8 seconds at first. In this case, just do what you can and build up your capacity over time.

I want you to remember something. You will never speak to anyone more than you speak to yourself in your own mind. So be sure to speak kind words. Learn how to be your own biggest cheerleader. Because that way, no one can ever bring you down. If you are forever going to allow the words, opinions, and actions of others to dictate how you feel and act, you'll never have any control over your own life. Learn to speak to yourself the same way you would to your best friend. Foster kindness and grace toward the most important person in your life, which is you. I know we like to tell ourselves it's our children or our spouse. That's bullshit. Stop doing that. The most important person in your life is you. Because if you don't look after yourself, what is left of yourself to give to your children or your spouse? You cannot pour from an empty cup, and there is also nothing wrong with:

- Being proud of yourself.
- Telling people that you're proud of yourself.
- Boasting about your accomplishments in a sincere manner. Not like a Karen.
- Just be yourself.

This is YOUR life! You do you. Stop comparing yourself to others because there is no comparison. There is only one Catherine Alexander Trimble-Lozano on planet Earth (you're welcome), and I'm learning to love myself!

And learn how to regulate your own emotions. It is the greatest gift anyone can give themselves. Without this skill, anyone can take your power from you at the drop of a hat.

"The greatest enemy will hide in the last place you would ever look."
- Julius Ceasar.

We always seek fault outside of ourselves when the answer lies within. What needs fixing lies within you. That's not to say that you're broken in any way. I'm just saying that we all have things we need to work on within ourselves, whether it be setting healthy boundaries, leading a healthy lifestyle, learning how to control our emotions, etc.

Perhaps one of the greatest pearls of wisdom I've received that's had a ginormous impact on my life is the realization that emotions aren't facts. They're just bits of information given to us by our nervous system in response to what's happening in and outside of us. You are not your emotions. You are not angry…you FEEL angry. You are not happy…you FEEL happy. In the same way that you can't MAKE someone else feel something, no one can MAKE you feel anything either. Yes, you might have an initial emotional response to something someone just did or said to you, but right after that, you get to CHOOSE what to do next. Remember, all you have to do is breathe.

Breathe and work on yourself, day in and day out. Take care of yourself, and the rest will follow.

Chapter 4

Super Momma

This chapter is for all my single working moms out there. I see you! I am you.

Dreaming about becoming a mom one day is a bit like a fairytale. You have these images in your mind of how wonderful it will be. Images that fill you with all kinds of warm, fuzzy feelings.

Becoming a mom is perhaps more than most women bargain for. It's not easy. It's hard as fuck sometimes. And when you're trying to do right by this little human that you created while juggling a stressful job and co-parenting all at the same time, I feel drawn to drugs and alcohol. I'm kidding—only a little.

No one tells you just how hard parenting can be. I don't think if anyone told me, it would've made much of a difference because you actually need to experience it to know what you're talking about. It's such an immense responsibility.

Raising a child is the only job on the planet where you work 24/7/365, and it costs you money instead of you getting paid. I recently had a group of moms chuckling when I said, "I wanted to be a mama. I wanted to do this. Being a mom is what I wanted," repeating it over and over. I had to remind myself of that multiple times when I was awoken by my alarm at 5 a.m. Saturday morning to get up and ready to take AJ to his chess tournament. AJ was being all grumppotamus because it was Saturday, and he didn't want to get up. Because, you know, I was so mean for making him get up so he could go to the tournament he wanted to participate in, and I paid for. It's a lose-lose many days, but dammit, I WANTED TO BE A MOM!

I honestly cannot fathom how women without support get by. I at least have a good stable job and amazing friends I can call on when in need. Then there are the mothers who work three jobs to give their children what they never had as a child. I salute you. Truly.

Recently, society has started referring to mothers as superheroes because we do everything. I don't know if the intent was to give us a backhanded compliment, but that's exactly what it is. It's a way of making women feel like we *have* to do it all; otherwise, it means we're a failure as a woman, wife, and mother. It's the same thing as when a husband states that he "helps" his wife with housework. You're not helping her asshat. It's your house, too. You're simply doing your part as part of a couple. You're not "helping" anyone. It's your fucking responsibility as well. I don't want to be a superhero. I mean teleportation and invisibility at my fingertips would be hella cool, but I'd far rather have proper support! Instead, I'm busy trying to figure out why my son's Occulus won't connect to the Wi-

Fi while coughing up a lung and crossing my legs, so I don't pee myself as I stand over the stove making dinner and simultaneously trying not to get fired as a result of pushing back on a budget in the online meeting I'm in with corporate executives. Spare me the carefully disguised misogyny.

You're expected to take care of all home duties. This includes cooking, cleaning, doing the laundry, figuring out what groceries are needed, going grocery shopping, fixing the kids' lunch, giving baths, dressing them, and tending to them when they get sick. Then you also need to take care of your partner, cook for the whole family, be ready to have sex (no headaches, ladies!) when it's expected of you, and not allow your hormones to influence you at all during PMS because then you're a moany bitch. Always be well groomed, do your job well, show up to parent/teacher meetings, volunteer at school, join community organizations so you can do your part, take care of your aging parents, and then die.

I'll never forget the day a female daycare worker at my son's school chirped about how sad it is that I have to travel so much, as it's causing me to miss out on so much of my son's life. Would she have said the same to me if I were a man? No! It would have likely sounded more like it's admirable that you sacrifice so much to provide for your family, sir. Well, guess what, Karen?? That's what I'm doing.

I shared a reel I saw recently with a number of my female friends where the woman speaking talked about all the responsibilities she has and how she wants to come back in her next life as a tree. Just resting and being beautiful and healthy. She further stated that once she's rested for a couple hundred years, she'd maybe be willing to come back as an uncle. Man did that shit resonate! I've often said I'm coming back as a dog of a good owner, but I'm rethinking that. I wanna be a tree!!

Then there was the PTA president, who shamed me because I couldn't make it to meetings on Tuesdays and Fridays at 10 a.m.—making me feel like a failure as a mom because of her own feeble-minded prejudices. Fuck you and the horse you rode in on, Karen. Okay, not the horse. I'm an animal lover. So just fuck you, Karen. It's not as though I'm out with friends getting mani/pedi's or on a ski trip to Vail. I'm running hospitals and trying to not fail miserably at raising a good human!

Who says women can't have it all? I don't know about you, but I have depression, anxiety, major mom guilt, an extra 35 lbs., debt, angst, and a soul-crushingly busy schedule! You can definitely have it all.

I must admit, I now finally understand why my folks had a ready-made pitcher of margaritas in their freezer when we were growing up. Parenting takes way more caffeine and alcohol than I could ever have imagined—holy mother of sanity.

Things have also changed a whole lot over the years. Do you ever start your day off by being chewed up and spit out, then body slammed to the floor verbally because you dared to wake up the little freeloader in your house to remind them that it's free dress day at school and to put on deodorant? No? Just me? Awesome.

AJ's in his tween years now, which means that I get a lot of eye rolls, grunting as answers to my questions, food wrappers and trash stashed in all the wrong places, and "I know, momma" when I remind him not to forget his backpack. Only to drive all the way to school and wait in the drop-off line to be told that he has, indeed, forgotten his backpack. Then you have to drive ALL the way back home and ALL the way back to the school again while you have a ton of work waiting for you at the office.

Then, I kid you not, he informed me when I picked him up that after all that, he'd gotten to school without his laptop and had detention tomorrow. I sometimes wonder whether he does it on purpose for shits and giggles.

Do other moms need to quit their full-time jobs just to keep up with all the emails from their kids' school and teachers? I mean, *this* teacher posts assignments in *this* app and *that* one in *that* app. If you want grades, that's on the parent portal. If you want math and science assignments, log into Schoology. If you want reading and writing work pending, log into Amplify! They all have different logins and passwords, and my ADHD son struggles to remember to put his name on papers, let alone to turn them in! But if I remind him, I get the "I know, mama" accompanied by a grunt. We're doomed.

I once heard Tina Fey say something along the lines of "I think every working single mom probably feels the same thing. You go through chunks of time where you're thinking, 'This is impossible, completely unrealistic, and impossible.' And then you just keep going and keep doing what you have to do, and you sort of just overcome the seemingly impossible somehow."

It really does feel impossible sometimes. Like you're drowning in all of these adulting responsibilities. I feel the memes stating, "adulting sucks, I want a refund," IN MY BONES! Sometimes I catch myself fantasizing about running away to some tropical island where I can lounge next to the ocean all day and have hot cabana boys fan me with palm leaves and serve me pina coladas.

But then the daydream bubble suddenly bursts because someone needs me. I wake up, and someone needs me. I get to work, and someone needs me. I get home, and someone needs me. There are dishes in the sink, clothes in the dryer for the third time today, baths to be taken, toys to be picked up, mouths to be fed, homework WWIII to be had, teachers to be emailed, a million school apps to be checked, lunches to be packed, etc. I'm not ignoring you. I'm just exhausted.

All while trying desperately not to make my favorite yoga pose be the downward spiral. Because that could easily happen, but we need to keep it together for everyone else, right?

Does anyone know when kids start listening? I mean, even if it's just an estimated ETA? Were we also little assholes at some stage in our parents' lives? Probably, I guess. I wish I had a manual that told me exactly what I needed to do to communicate with my son sometimes. When I do something magical in AJ's eyes, he says, "Wow, momma. How did you know this or that." My go-to response is I learned that in mommy school. When I regrettably really screw up, I own it and apologize, and I just about died laughing the time AJ asked me if I'd missed that day at mommy school!! He was 3! Sadly, there is no mommy school. Also, I did *not* get the memo on preparing myself for the puberty boy odor that I'd be subjecting my nostrils to. I mean, what is that? All my boy mommas out there, you know what I mean. It's like a swampy smell mixed with a bit of body odor and a tinge of butthole. Man, alive! It never ceases to amaze me how I can smell my son's armpits from 20 feet away, but he can't smell it when it's literally 6 inches from his nose. I've never been able to understand that in a hospital setting, either. We love our patients as those in healthcare service for the right reasons do… But then there's that old saying/advice about always wearing clean underwear and wiping well because you never know when you could be in an accident and end up in the emergency department. Is it a case that you get so used to your own odor that your nose just doesn't register the fumes awaiting some innocent, unsuspecting nose, probably attached to a poor nurse?

It's a constant balancing act between keeping the peace and being about 3 seconds away from completely losing your shit. However, when your little one is experiencing big emotions and loses their shit, you have to remain calm and remind yourself that he's not equipped to handle such big emotions yet. He's still learning. He's going through the motions like we've all had to. His brain is literally not even fully developed yet, so how can I possibly expect him to react in a manner that resembles maturity? That would be unfair. It doesn't stop me from wanting to shout back sometimes, and I have a fully developed adult brain. If you've never had to carry your screaming child out of a store, surfboard style, have you even really parented?

It reminds me of one of my all-time favorite movie scenes from Jerry Maguire, where he says to Rod, "*I am out here for you. You don't know what it's like to be ME out here for YOU. It is an up-at-dawn, pride-swallowing siege that I will never fully tell you about, OK? Help me! Help me, help you!*" I'd say that pretty much sums up what it is like attempting not to fail miserably at motherhood. And boy, is it ever a pride-swallowing, soul-devouring daily struggle not to just throat punch the little one. But then there are those briefest moments of hope when you're "momma" and not "bruh." When they say they love you and thank you. We remember they are worth it all in just that one brief moment.

And, of course, there are times when you'll fail. We all do at some point, and that's okay. It's funny how you can be having the worst day ever. Even directly related to your child. But then they turn around and tell you they love you or say, "Thank you, momma" and hug you, and you melt. It's getting to work and going to put your sunglasses away only to find a rock or a pinecone stuck in that compartment. It's cringing and trying not to explode or completely lose your shit when your expensive shampoo/conditioner/perfume bottle has been completely emptied into the tub because they made a magic potion they couldn't wait to show you! I laughed out loud reading this on someone's post the other day because it's *exactly* what motherhood is like. "*I was in a very bad mood today. Then my 3-year-old walked over, handed me a rock, patted my face, and said, "Mommy, you're perfect. Here's a present for you. And I smiled. Then I looked down and realized the rock was a cat turd".* I can so relate!

And after all is said and done, I wouldn't change it for the world. Yes, it is hard as fuck sometimes, and I've been to the brink of madness and back more times than I care to admit. I remember being at one of AJ's swim meets one day, sitting in the stands cheering him on. He looked up at one point, scanning the bleachers and looking for me. When our eyes met, he lit up, and the biggest smile appeared on his face. That moment hit me, and I had tears welling in my eyes. I realized then he wasn't looking for the perfect mother; he was just looking for his momma.

Life as a single mother has pushed me to my limits but has also taught me so much about myself, my child, parenthood, and life in general. It is quite the journey we get to walk as guardians of these little humans we've created. It truly is a magnificent blessing, no matter how hard it can be at times.

As a child, I often scanned the bleachers, and my parents weren't there. I did have the parents of fellow band members who treated me as their own, though. My parents were often too busy, with my dad having evening work obligations as a musician and my mom having my little brother at home needing a little extra effort and attention. I was left to figure out how to be my own cheerleader. How to be the strong one who could, would, and did always figure things out for herself. That little girl inside of me still wishes to see my parents cheering me on in the bleachers when I look up, scanning for them.

Childhood trauma (any trauma) causes changes within you that you didn't choose. Healing from it is all about finally getting to practice your right to choose what you want to change. I think it is important to share that it took me a lot of reading, writing, and therapy to understand that there are many different types of trauma that can have a profound effect on us. When someone would describe what I'd shared as traumatic, I'd almost feel guilty thinking it wasn't as though I were chained up or starved or something. Trauma doesn't have to be extreme physical or sexual abuse. The trauma of extremely stressful or distressing events and living situations can have huge implications later in life when we don't have appropriate and effective coping mechanisms.

I want to be the best parent I can possibly be for my boy. Perfection is not an option, but neither is failure! I know that aiming for perfection is a sure way of setting myself up for failure. None of us are perfect. However, I figure that if you choose to act from a place of love, understanding, and support daily, then you're winning at parenthood.

Give yourself some grace. No one has it all figured out, and you don't have to either. Life is hard enough as it is without us adding to the pile. You can only carry so much – and if it gets too heavy, it's okay to rest. Set it down and catch your breath in whichever way you need to. You cannot pour from an empty cup. You cannot be your best for your children unless you look after yourself first. I know we're taught differently, but it is just simple mathematics. If you have two energy points and your child needs three, sorry, momma. It's not going to happen. I know. I know you'd give your life, as would I. But that doesn't serve them either.

Mom first, then stinky bum. Self-love and self-care aren't optional. It's crucial for your survival. Especially when you have some idiots and assholes to contend with at work on top of everything else.

Chapter 5

Idiot to Asshole Ratio

SOME DAYS REQUIRE MORE THAN OTHERS

FUCK OFF SPRAY KEEP FUCKTARDS AWAY FOR UP TO 4 HOURS

SPRAY DIRECTLY INTO THE FACE OF FUCKTARD

ALWAYS KEEP A CAN AROUND

How many idiots and or assholes do you come face-to-face with in your life on a daily basis? I bet it's more than we care to openly acknowledge, right? And is it just me or did this get far worse post pandemic?? I would think after everyone being locked in their houses living life in their own four walls folks would be happy to be out and about. Unfortunately though it seems like patience and acceptance is at an all time low! People will flip their lid over the smallest of inconveniences.

You're probably wondering, "What the hell is an idiot-to-asshole ratio?" My Dad talked about this often and explained it to me one day when I was super frustrated regarding a situation in my career. The idea is that you can be successful, both in business and in life, as an idiot OR as an asshole. But not both.

An idiot can be successful if they are kind, caring, and good at building relationships and loyalty because people will like them and want to work hard for them. An asshole, on the other hand, can be greatly successful if they really know their shit. They can execute ideas and projects to bring in strong results, which is the only thing that many corporate executives and board members care about. People will put up with an asshole because of what they bring to the table, but only for as long as they deliver.

I used to buy into the idea that you cannot be both until I met someone who proved that hypothesis wrong by excelling in both. Someone who was both completely out of their league, title, and role AND was also a complete asshole. How? You ask. I call it *"weaponized incompetence."* When you find yourself in the precarious position of working for and reporting to someone who is both an idiot and an asshole, may God have mercy on your soul because they will make your life a living hell! Instead of your ideas and experience being leveraged to their and the company's advantage and that of the team's, you WILL be perceived as a threat and identified as a target. Both idiots and assholes intrinsically fear those who are both competent and sure of themselves. I like to call this the weaponization of incompetence. They set a negative narrative about you at the top and spin your every move to match their story….and man alive are they good at it! Sadly before you know what happened, you go from being on every committee with a seat at the decision-making table, to an enemy of the state. The performance of your market and the incredible successes of you and your team are overlooked and explained away. It becomes as though you're public enemy number one and despite the strong relationships with the worker bees at corporate, the executive leadership is slowly but strategically poisoned against you.

I've worked in corporate America and at the executive level long enough to know that you want the best and brightest on your team. If I'm the smartest person in the room, "*Houston, we have a problem.*" You want people to bring expertise that you don't have to the table. The mark of a true leader is the ability to bring the best out of the people who are on their team. The ability to motivate, encourage, push, and support.

An invaluable lesson I've learned as a woman in business and executive leadership is that those who try to make your life hell don't hate you. They hate that despite all their efforts to bring you down and destroy you, you've not allowed it to affect you, and you're still thriving. That despite all their efforts, you are still admired and looked up to by your counterparts. You are still loved by your team. You aren't afraid to challenge ideas or to stand up for yourself when necessary. It's the typical bully mindset. What they want most is for you to show fear and crumble at the sight of them. Bullies and assholes are cut from the same cloth. Another thing they have in common is that a deep sense of insecurity drives their behavior. It's the same with narcissists. I feel like these are all synonyms. However, we have started using the term "narcissist" too willy-nilly in recent years, in my opinion.

You see, assholes only have one game plan or one card up their sleeve. Do whatever it takes to look good in the eyes of those who write your paycheck, and throw those who oppose you under the bus as soon as possible. The moment they can no longer deliver because their team has been annihilated or because the powers that be finally see them for who they truly are, the jig is up. Do not pass go. Do not collect two hundred dollars.

Those who are competent and want to see the team succeed will always elevate those around them. Did you know that a study conducted showed that if you find yourself sitting within a 25-foot radius of a low performer, it will bring your performance down by up to 30%? On the flip side, if you sit within 25 feet of a high performer, your performance will go up by 15%.

In the same way, research conducted by the authors of the book Thinkfluence has shown that you are 57% more likely to become obese if you have an obese friend. 40% if you have a sibling who is obese, and 37% if your spouse is obese. These are pretty scary statistics, but this is where sayings like "you are the average of the five people you spend the most time with" come from. And the research shows that it's true. This is why it's so crucial that you choose who you allow into your circle very carefully. Bring on the badass, brilliantly successful, ethical, lovingly supportive, loyal women!

This is also why both an idiot and an asshole can't and won't survive in the same place for too long. They either replace the competent players with weak "yes people" to do their bidding without question. Or they inevitably affect those around them, causing key players and valuable members to leave, eventually causing the system to collapse. One bad apple can indeed spoil the bunch or the whole damn company.

Anywhere I am in a position of authority or when I own my own company, my team and I will continue to intentionally hire people who are smarter and more talented than ourselves to increase the value of the team and their performance. Having access to people who are smarter than you and better at different things than you is an absolute blessing. Not a threat.

What your title or position is in a company doesn't matter. What matters is how you treat people. The great Maya Angelou phrased it perfectly, saying, "*I've learned that people will forget what you said, people will forget what you did, but people will never forget how you made them feel.*" It's so true, isn't it?

Never learning to spell my name right is a great example. Allie. I mean, it's not some thirty-syllable word with different accent marks and symbols. But it's Allie. Not Ali, like my neighbor's bulldog. Not Alley, as in the small road running behind my house. It's Allie. And your absolute refusal to spell it correctly in written communication is rude! But also don't fake it. Don't tell me that you're concerned about my travel having a negative impact on "MJ". My son's name is "AJ" and we're doing just fine. Thank you very much. These little details are important, and when missed they have a big impact on morale! As the little girl on Full House used to say. *"It makes someone feel unimportant."*

Or how about in a meeting with all the leaders and various people present when the boss says, "not to call anyone out, but (totally calls someone out)"? Another big sign of an idiot asshole is the person who praises in private and chastises publicly. Not cool.

I cringe when people say it's not a popularity contest. You're right, it isn't. It's a responsibility you take on. It comes with the so-called coveted title you've accepted. With great power comes great responsibility, as Uncle Ben would tell you. You're right, Karen! In fact, it's not a contest at all! These are people's LIVES you're playing with when you're stuck in your puny ego, trying to make examples of people so you'll feel more powerful because you know that, in reality, you're a weak asshole.

When a real leader walks into a room, the followers feel intimidated, the snakes feel threatened, and the future leaders feel inspired. For those in leadership roles, how do you make people feel when you walk into a room?

I will always aim to be the kind of leader I'd want to work with and for. The one who spells my damn name correctly for starters. The type that knows my son's name. The boss that asks how my father's treatment is going. When everything goes right, I give all the credit to those on my team and when things go wrong, I stand between them and the firing squad to take the hit. I circle back and apologize when I inevitably get it wrong. I love when the illustrious Betty White said, *"Why do people say,*

'Grow some balls'? Balls are weak and sensitive. If you really wanna get tough, grow a vagina. Those things can really take a pounding!"

Another thing I see a lot of in the workplace is the insecurities among female leaders. Most have had to work so hard and sacrifice so much to get to where they are that they instantly feel threatened when another strong woman comes along. We need to stop that kind of nonsense and work to raise one another up.

Women actually run the world, sweetheart. I mean, even Beyoncé says so! There's no need for you to feel threatened. Team up instead. Men think with their big egos and tiny penises. Women think with their brains and their hearts. Our balls were put on our chests because they were way too big to fit between our legs, remember?

Together, we will always trump single-minded assholiness.

You are powerful and a force to be reckoned with. Now, straighten that crown and go get yours!

Chapter 6

But Did You Die?

I think there's a fine line in striking a balance between giving yourself grace and tough love. My fellow nurses here are likely familiar with the whole "but did you die?" point of view. It's a mix of dark humor, survival skills, and sarcasm! One of my favorite Meredith Grey lines is, "You can have the worst crap in the world happen to you, and you can get over it. All you gotta do is survive". Hence the "but did you die"?!?

A mother, especially, doesn't have the luxury of curling up in a ball and shutting the world out when life becomes too much. Thank God that we women never get a "man cold." Just imagine! The whole world would cease to rotate on its axis! Self-care can often feel like a luxury when it's actually a necessity. Where do you fit it in, though? I've learned that you have to make time to fit it in; otherwise, it won't happen, and you'll be burned out with no other option than to curl up in a ball and shut the world out. If you don't make time for your health and well-being, illness will do it for you. It's tough, but it's true.

When we're children, we always look to our parents for a responsive queue when we fall down. When AJ was little, the first thing he'd do when he fell down was look for me to see how I reacted, then base his response on my reaction. One day, he fell down and looked around to locate me, only to find me yelling, "You're safe," and gesturing like a baseball umpire, making the base run call as he lay on the floor. He'd then get back up and carry on. If I gasped and ran over saying, "Oh, sweety pie. Are you okay?" He'd start bawling and losing his mind over his scraped knee. I got really good at the umpire gesturing while raising this boy!

This is how we build up resilience. You stumble, fall, learn, and get back up and do it better if you're lucky enough to have the wherewithal to look for the lesson. Otherwise, you'll soon be right back in the same place you were. Congratulations, you get a do-over until you learn the lesson. If you don't, you'll remain in the same loop all your life.

The beauty (and bane) of being an adult is having freedom of choice. You either *choose* to stay down when you stumble and fall, or you *choose* to get back up. You either *choose* to focus on your own development by going to therapy and putting in the work to heal, or you *choose* to remain ignorant and repeat the same pattern ad infinitum.

It can take a lifetime to learn when you need to take a bubble bath and when you need to tell yourself to "suck it up, buttercup." Or perhaps the secret ingredient is combining the two. There's a thought. You can sit in a bubble bath, sipping wine, and tell yourself to suck it up. Because women can have it all, right? There we go.

Jokes aside, though, self-compassion is so important in this sometimes overwhelmingly cruel life. You need to be the adult you needed when you were a little girl. You need to remember who the fuck you are while also realizing that there's a girl inside of you who carries a lot of hurt. Even if you might not admit it to anyone, I know. I know what it's like to suck it up for a lifetime. But honey, let me tell you, sooner or later, it will bite you in the ass unless you do the inner work needed. Do the work so you don't perpetuate generational trauma. Do the work so you don't end up a bitter, resentful old lady sucking her thumb and rocking back and forth in the corner. Do the work so you can become the woman you've always dreamed of. Do the work so you can take care of that little girl inside of you the way she always wished someone would. Do the work because you're worth it. You've always been worth it. You will always be worth it.

We are pow-HER-ful when we overcome everything that is meant to destroy us. Nothing will hit harder in life than life itself. Guaranteed that we'll all go through some semblance of adversity at one point or another. You don't always have control over what happens to you. What you do have control over is what you choose to do with what happens to you.

Focusing on the things outside of your control is like buying yourself a one-way ticket to mental illness and heartache. You can do nothing to change the things that are outside your control. So, why spend your time worrying about it? Focus on what you can control. What are those?

- You can control who you allow into your life.

- You can control the boundaries you set with others and teach them how you want to be treated.

- You can control what you put into your body.

- You can control the content you allow yourself to consume online.

- You can control the amount of exercise you make time for. *(Not preaching here, as anyone who knows me knows I'm not running unless something is chasing me)*

- You can control the thoughts you allow yourself to focus on.

- You can control the emotions you allow yourself to get caught up in.

- You can control your self-discipline.

- You can control how you choose to react to whatever happens to you.

- You can control your beliefs.

- You can control whether to invest in learning or not.

- You can control your attitude.

- You can control the effort you put into things.

- You can control how you speak to yourself.

You cannot control the following:

- You cannot control what others think of you.

- You cannot always control what happens to you.

- You cannot control how others behave.

- You cannot control the weather.

- You cannot control other people's beliefs.

- You cannot control other people's values.

- You cannot control how others respond to you.

- You cannot control the news.

- You cannot control others' feelings.

- You cannot control what will happen.

If you spend all your energy on the things you cannot control, you'll have no resources left to invest in all the things you can. This is when your life feels out of control because it's exactly that. You've taken your free choice and given it to something you cannot control.

Choose to focus your finite daily energy on the things in your life you can control. This way, you'll learn more, build more resilience, and be in control of your life. Even if the world around you may be in chaos, this is how you remain calm amid the storm.

This way, when you fall, you won't have to look for someone to guide how you should react because you're in control. You can say, "*You're safe!*" and signal the umpire base call for your damn self!

Chapter 7

TGIFF (Thank God it's Fucking Friday)

The average person will spend about 90,000 hours at work over their lifetime. That's about a third of your life. ONE THIRD of your precious life on this planet is spent earning enough money so you can actually live. Some may call it work-life balance. There's no such thing. If we wait to live only on weekends, we'll miss the whole point of living.

It's not work-life balance. It's LIFE balance. I remember sitting on a panel of senior healthcare executives and being asked how I ensure my work-life balance. I chuckled and said, "*I admit to myself and others that work-life balance is bullshit.*" There's no such thing. Some days, work wins, and some days, friends and family win. In the end, my prayer is that it balances out. The truth is I am one person and cannot always be all things to everyone. It's impossible. I work really hard to pick exceptional people to be part of my team. The A-Team, I call it. Because when talented folks are bought in, they help achieve the goals and ultimate success, and they are able to step in and step up at any time. And they have. I've been so incredibly grateful for the team I have built because their knowledge, experience, and work ethic have allowed me to still be there for my dad during his cancer journey and have the time to make it to more of the special events for AJ that I'd otherwise have to miss out on. Don't get me wrong. I don't make them all, but I wouldn't make any if I didn't have the team I have! And if I don't make it, my badass mom friends are there to cheer on AJ and send me pics and videos, so I don't miss out on the memories all together!

What's crucial is that, as with every other part of our lives, we need to set and enforce strong boundaries that allow us to invest the limited time we have enjoying the things we value in life. Come Friday, when I've been putting up with all sorts of bullshit all week, don't talk to me unless you're asking me whether I want it neat or on the rocks. If you don't set these boundaries, people will take advantage of your free time. Is your work really worth it? The regular weekend text from your boss to all their direct reports requesting X, Y & Z to them by Sunday so they have time to review it all by Monday. Um, sorry, but your lack of planning and communication does not constitute an emergency on my part.

This is why it's so important to find something that you love. This way, it's not work; it's your passion. How does the saying by Mark Twain go? *"Find something you enjoy doing, and you'll never have to work a day in your life."*

I absolutely love my job because I love my team. But some days, work wins, and some days, another part of my life wins. Work-life balance just doesn't exist. There will be days when I need to spend more time than I'd like on work stuff because it's needed, part of my job, and part of my responsibilities. Other days, work might not be as demanding, and I get to invest more time and energy into spending more time with AJ or my friends.

What I have learned is you must NEVER ask, "*What else?*" You know what I'm talking about. When you're having one of those days. Those days when everything just seems to pile onto an already unmanageable heap of shit, and you throw your arms in the air, asking, "*What else?*" At that moment, God or the Universe WILL answer by showing you EXACTLY what else could go wrong. Don't tempt fate.

It reminds me of my dad saying his sister taught him never to pray for patience but rather grace. I guess the idea is that if you pray for patience, you'll continue to be challenged endlessly to build your threshold. If you pray for grace, you get better at handling what comes your way.

I never learn lessons the easy way. I'm stubborn like that. I'm going to need you to tell me ten or a million times. I'm going to need to try 20 different ways and fall flat on my face, and then maybe just a couple more. But maybe if I do it this way, it will work. No? Okay, how about this way? Maybe some grace WAS given because lucky for me, I learned this particular lesson a couple of years ago and without the bonk on the head normally required. I was officing out of one of the urgent care centers I oversaw and got an urgent call from one on the other side of town that fell under my purview. A nurse of mine was in a really toxic relationship. Nurses often become nurses because we're "fixers." We want to fix and heal the world. So, we often end up in codependent narcissistic relationships because these types of people are so good at preying on compassionate empaths.

This particular nurse's excuse for a boyfriend had sucker punched her in the parking lot, and police were en route. I got in my car and flew up and over the mountain, separating the two locations, only to be pulled over for speeding as I was preparing to exit the freeway. I explained the situation to the police officer, and after about ten minutes and a hefty fine (insert eye roll), he let me be on my way.

I got to the urgent care and was attempting to console the team that had witnessed the assault and were all shaken up. Trying to convince the nurse to press charges and make a change in her life. As I was standing there, I started getting labor pains as I was nine months pregnant at the time as well. I looked up and said really? Now? What else? As those words escaped my mouth, I was called and informed that an elderly man had just driven into the urgent care center I'd just left to respond to this crisis. When I say drove in, there's no drive-thru line! I mean, he hit the gas instead of the brake, hopped the curb, and drove his vehicle into the building! Needless to say, I've NEVER again looked up and said what else! Sometimes, I will look up and say I know you must need the entertainment, so I hope y'all are enjoying this. I like to picture my friends and family who have gone before me sitting at their favorite pub in heaven, getting a real belly laugh over whatever I'm trying to navigate. I love the idea of my Mimi, who used to say, "Alex…you have absolutely no personality, and you look like a toad", sitting there loving the witty, snarky in a good way, sometimes all-out smart ass, sassy granddaughter I turned out to be! This was the day that TGIF became TGIFF for me, as I went out on bed rest for the last ten days of pregnancy!

Fun times.

I think it's just a testament to the fact that if you ask God, the Universe, Buddha, or whatever you believe in something, he/she/they/it will answer. If you're asking for patience to deal with the challenges yet to come into your life, what you're focusing on is the challenges that are yet to come into your life. Rather, focus on asking for the things you want, like grace, a good life, good health, self-discipline, and a partner who loves you and wants what's best for you, even if that means pushing you and challenging you to become the best version of yourself. Certainly not someone like that sad excuse of a man who would take his inability to regulate his own emotions out on a defenseless woman.

We already spend so much time at a job we've chosen to take on to survive in a world driven by money.

What's really interesting is that, during the COVID-19 pandemic, an unprecedented 47 million Americans voluntarily quit their jobs and exited the job market during what is now known as the "Great Resignation." Why? Because it took a life-threatening pandemic to get people to stop for a moment and realize that they weren't happy in their jobs. When you're put in a situation like full-on lockdown with a deadly virus that stares you in the face and reminds you of your own fragility and mortality, it makes you revise the status quo.

Is it really worth sacrificing your life, doing something you don't (at least) enjoy doing so that you can etch out something that looks like merely surviving?

If I ask you, "What does it mean to live?" what would your answer be? Think about it for a minute.

We so easily get caught up in the frazzling pace of the rat race that it takes something momentous to remind us to stop now and again and take stock of our lives. Are you doing what you want to be doing? Are you content with your life? Should you be making some changes?

I think the point of this life is to exercise our God-given free will to make smart choices on a daily basis so we get to a place where we don't have to say TGIFF.

Build a life you don't have to or want to take a break from. Since we only get one shot at this particular life, isn't that what we should all focus on? ***YOLO!***

Chapter 8

Use Your Words

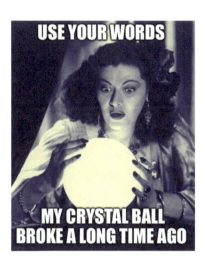

I believe that so much of human suffering could be prevented if we were all just taught how to communicate effectively. It always boggles my mind that this is not taught in our schools. I think our education syllabus needs a proper overhaul as it's still based on our needs as a society at the break of the industrial age. Things have changed—a lot. The way we teach our children and the skills the educational system focuses on imparting to them also need updating. And for the love of God, can we PLEASE get rid of this "new" math bullshit? Asking for a friend.

If everyone were just taught how to communicate effectively, it would prevent so many misunderstandings and solve many of our problems. Later in this book, you'll be introduced to a period in my life that I call "the dumpster fire of online dating." It's that period in a woman's life post-divorce when you're delusional enough to think that online dating might be worth a shot.

I met this one guy who, at first, I didn't realize was doing the whole covert communication thing with me. My crystal ball broke a *long* time ago. So, you need to give it to me straight. Use your words to help me understand what you want to communicate, or take your pouting elsewhere.

This dude, whom I've given the alias "Hola" (I'll explain it later), sends me a text of the song "It Takes Two" by Rob Base and DJ EZ Rock. I love that song! So, I reply, saying, "Great song! Love that one!" It took forever to dawn on me that this guy was trying to communicate that he felt like I wasn't contributing as much as he'd like to this casual dating relationship we had going on. And by casual dating relationship, I mean ONE group date set up by a friend couple who also knew him and ONE unsupervised dinner at a chain restaurant. But instead of USING HIS WORDS, he sends me a song. Because, you know, telepathy is such a common phenomenon. How about, no?!

I see it all the time in my friends' relationships with their significant others, at work within different teams, within families, and within friend circles. People don't use their words, and then this burning ball of resentment builds up inside them. They're sour pusses because the person they've been dropping subtle hints to hasn't used their magical powers to pick up on the message and fall to their knees apologizing. I mean, instead of huffing and puffing and being all pissed off about it, how about just saying, "*Can you please put the toilet seat down so that I don't get an unexpected bidet experience when I need to pee in the middle of the night.*" Now, if you say that multiple times and your ass continues to get an unrequested bath when you use the restroom, then pissed off it is, and I say throat punch!

We live in a world where communication has changed so much over such a short period of time. We've gone from conversations around the dinner table with the family every night to sitting in front of the television on our phones as we eat our fast food, seeking connection anywhere other than where our feet are planted.

The anonymity of online communication has given rise to a whole new breed of bullies and keyboard warriors who take their insecurities out on anyone who crosses their online browser. A dear friend, also known as "Greece," calls this phenomenon keyboard courage. It's easy to say hard things via text. Good and bad.

Children and teens don't know how to have an in-person conversation (and God forbid we want eye contact) because they spend most of their time communicating with their friends online through online gaming platforms or texting apps. Hell, their entire school experience is now on the computer, whether they are at school physically or otherwise! So many young people prefer to communicate electronically these days. So perhaps it means I'm young since I'd nearly always prefer you to text me? I'm that person who will actively text you for hours on end and then not answer, staring at my phone when you call. I need to dive into that phenomenon. I wonder what deep-seated root issue I may find for that one. What does that mean for relationships? How do you express your thoughts and feelings within a relationship with a real person? By texting them when they're sitting right next to you? Perhaps a string of emoji's? I mean really!

I feel like we're raising a generation that's become so inept at facing and dealing with their own emotions (because they prefer to distract themselves with social media) that it affects their resilience in a major way. I'm sorry to break it to you flower, but not all places of work have a "safe space" room for your fragile days.

I used to think communication was key. Communication is only one part of the equation to understanding. Comprehension of what is being communicated is the second, maybe more important, part of that equation. You can communicate all you want with someone, but if they don't understand you or choose not to hear what it is you're saying, it's like talking to a wall. But, if you don't at least try to explain by using your words, it's hopeless. Part of the issue here is that in this fast-paced tech environment, people no longer listen to understand. To comprehend. They listen simply to respond, which really isn't listening at all.

According to Project.co's annual report on communication statistics, a whopping 42% of people said that they had suffered from burnout due to communication issues in their business or workplace. Imagine what that statistic might look like within romantic relationships where there's an even stronger emotional screen through which we communicate.

I'm sure you've heard or read somewhere that most of our human communication happens nonverbally. Albert Mehrabian, professor emeritus of psychology at the University of California, was the first person to break down the different components of a face-to-face conversation into percentages. His research found that 55% of our communication is nonverbal, 38% is vocal, and only 7% is words alone.

With such a small percentage of our communication depending on the words we use; it is obvious that using your words, is a crucial aspect of effective communication. Especially because so much of our communication happens over the phone or online. Mr. Hola wasn't standing in front of me when he sent me that song, so there was no way for me to read his body language. The only information I had to go on was a link to a song, which, for all intents and purposes, could've just been sent for fun because he liked the song. That's what I initially thought, anyway, as I jammed out in the carpool line singing away, "*It takes two to make a thing go right.*" Oops!

University of Wisconsin's Professors Scott, Cutlip, and Allen published their book introducing the now-famous 7 Cs of Communication in 1952. It is a system developed to help anyone communicate more effectively. According to the 7 Cs, communication needs to be:

- Clear.

- Concise.

- Concrete.

- Correct.

- Coherent.

- Complete.

- Courteous.

How many people do you know who can communicate effectively in this manner?

As I get older, I'm also beginning to realize that maturity greatly impacts a person's ability to communicate effectively. If you have a 40-something-year-old on your team with the maturity level of a 16-year-old, they won't be able to comprehend what you're trying to communicate, nor accept it for what it is.

I honestly don't know how to communicate with immature individuals because it's useless. I mean, if I need to bust out the crayons, I'm out! You try to help and do your best, but they can only take on board what their maturity level allows them. The same goes for people with limited or fixed mindsets. If someone focuses their attention on all that is doom and gloom, they'll start believing that all is doom and gloom and there's nothing you can say to change their mind. I call them energy vampires. They will suck the joy right out of you.

I learned this neat, easy-to-remember 4-step communication technique that seems to work really well. When you want to communicate something to someone, always use "I feel" language. The four steps go like this:

"I feel…"

"When you…"

"Because…"

"Next time, please…"

So, as a real-world example, it may sound something like this:

"I feel excluded."

"When you ignore my contributions in meetings."

"Because I think I have inputs that can be of value."

"Next time, please be mindful not to ignore me when I'm trying to communicate my ideas."

See? It's really not that hard. I know our feelings can be uncomfortable, and we sometimes fear how the other person may react, but, honey, let me tell you, miscommunication will cost you far more than just using your words. Plus, I feel it is *far* easier for someone else to digest and potentially incorporate change from this rather than one from a more accusatory stance. Imagine saying in the above example, "*You always ignore my input and devalue my contributions. You need to change that.*" I don't know about you, but if I were on the receiving end of these statements, I'd take much more kindly to the one expressed as a feeling rather than an "accusation." Just be ready for that boss, friend, or family member who deflects with the "you take things too personally" or "you're too emotional" retort. Barf, and shame on them! You need to be mindful in your personal life of those you find yourself doing this with repeatedly on the same topic. They're either incapable of or unwilling to change, and the ball is in your court to determine how you move forward. Peace over drama and distance over disrespect! Afterall, kindness is my go to, but fuck off is my wingman!

Try it out. You can thank me later.

Chapter 9

When Pigs Fly

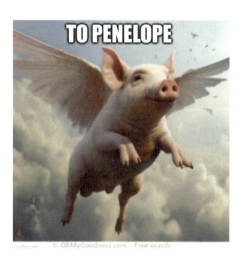

"It only seems impossible until it is done."
- Nelson Mandela.

My team knows exactly what I mean when I say "Penelope." One of my Allie-isms is giving a crystal pig with wings in a little glass dome to the leaders when they join my team. It's become my code-word for those situations where it seems like what we're shooting for is perhaps just outside of the realm of possibility. You know, it's those times when you have an impossible deadline staring you down. Or how about the time during Covid when oxygen deliveries were delayed and we rolled out liquid oxygen in an effort to save patients. I received a phone call from my then boss telling me I'd be fired if I'd damaged any of the hospital systems with my "nonsense". I'll have you know that not only was I not fired, but liquid o2 was rolled out nationally. No kudos necessary though because we did it to save lives, not gain favor. I'll admit, a sorry I was wrong and apology for the threat of termination would have been nice, but to each their own. That's when I'll say "Penelope." When the odds are stacked against us, but here we go because it's the right thing to do! Because we will soar in the face of adversity or any scenario that has you saying, "That'll happen the day pigs fly." Codeword Penelope for *we'll see it done.*

I have faced a lot of doubt and judgment from people in my life. Mainly because I'm the kind of person who goes after what she wants, and I don't subscribe to the notion of anything not being possible for me just because I'm a woman, a single mom, or not independently wealthy. When you put in a lot of work to achieve things most people only dream of, a trail of resentment usually follows. Funny, because most of those who resent your achievements and struggle to celebrate your successes are also the folks I call the coat-tail people. If you didn't have the time or the resources to support me when I was plain old Allie, don't come calling when it's Allie with initials. If you didn't believe in me and support me in my growth endeavors when I was Allie RN (registered nurse), then please continue in your lack of belief in Allie CEO. Same Allie, same you. Buh-bye now.

The same goes the other way, too, however. Some people sadly forget all of those who supported and cheered them on along their journey. They become successful, and rather than building and pulling others up with them, they stop responding or even push you down. Sadly, this seems more of a female thing as men make introductions and support each other. They call their buddy Bill, the President at such and such a company, have lunch at the country club, and devise a plan to get the other guy into that new VP seat. Women? Sadly, not so much. Let's change that!

I've learned that when someone looks at me and judges what I aim to achieve, they tell me that it's not possible or "Sure, when pigs can fly," it actually has nothing to do with me.

We all project our inner state of being upon others. When someone tells you that you're not capable of doing something, it's because they don't believe themselves to be capable of doing that something. And because they can't fathom themselves doing it, surely *you're* unable to, right? Because, in that person's mind, if you can achieve something they can't, they allow themselves to have that make them feel small and insignificant. This is what causes people to tell you you can't do something. They don't think they can achieve it and don't want you to achieve it either.

I'm what you'd call an overachiever. People who are 'fixers' are often seen as overachievers. We want to accomplish it all. We want to live our dreams and fix all the world's problems along the way. It's a trait that's often born from early childhood adversity or childhood trauma. Another tell-tale symptom of being an overachiever is the inability to stop and rest for a minute. We're always chasing a goal and don't know how to stop and stand still for a second. Take a break. Do nothing. Achieving the impossible? Sure, watch this. Sit still and do nothing for 5 minutes? Yeah, that'll happen the day pigs can fly.

We place way too much value on the opinions of others. Why, in God's name, would you allow someone else's insecurities to keep you from living your dreams? I'll tell you why: it's because of your own insecurities or low sense of self-worth—another tell-tale sign of adverse childhood experiences.

When our parents or primary caregivers don't show up for us in a way that teaches us that we're worthy of love, attention, understanding, and their time, it often translates into a lifelong struggle with a low sense of self-esteem. It's often more of a subconscious core belief that impacts every aspect of one's life. Often, the course of your life that you credit as fate is not that at all. It is the culmination of an endless number of subconscious choices you make based on previous experiences and thoughts. Nothing fateful about it. Just your own subconscious thoughts ruling your behavioral choices.

It takes a lot of time, effort, money, and tears to do the inner work needed to get to where you can turn the "Impossible" into "I'm Possible." Taking chances is scary. But something else should scare you more than anything—missing out on something truly wonderful because you allowed doubt and fear to keep you from taking a leap.

As George Bernard Shaw would put it: "*People who say it cannot be done should not interrupt those who are doing it.*"

It's usually the people who are crazy enough to think that they can change the world who end up doing so. (Quote by Steve Jobs)

You start to learn grace when you realize that people's behavior has nothing to do with you but everything to do with the internal struggles and demons they're dealing with on a daily basis. It changes the narrative in your mind from "What is wrong with me?" to "Wow…poor them!"

I think this also very much links in with one's ability to regulate their own emotions. So few people are even aware that they're not dealing with their emotions as effectively as they could, never mind having an awareness of the need to change. And then there's also the fact that most people don't want to change. They don't want to accept accountability for their own actions. It's far easier to blame their woes on something external to them.

Later, I will address people saying, "You are intimidating." No, you FEEL intimidated, and now you're blaming something external to you (me) rather than owning up to your own insecurities.

If you want to achieve the seemingly impossible and get through those when pigs fly types of situations in your life, you need to take accountability for what is within your control. You can't achieve the seemingly impossible if you always focus on everything and everyone on the outside. There's very little that you can control outside of yourself. You need to turn your focus inward. Learn how to control what thoughts you allow yourself to focus on a daily basis. Because if others are telling you that you're incapable, and you're telling yourself the same thing– well, I've got news for you. You're not capable.

You will always attract more of what you focus on. Have you ever thought about wanting to buy a truck? You have a truck in mind. Maybe it's a Ford F150. Suddenly, you start spotting Ford F150s everywhere you go. Or okay, ladies…how about when you think you might be pregnant but haven't tested yet? Every commercial is for formula or diapers! Every woman you pass on the street is pushing a stroller or carrying an infant in a papoose. There's a big baby shower invitation posted in the lounge! Who's with me?

Or let's say all you focus on all day is how little time you have to do what you need to get done. It never feels like you have enough time. Why? Because you keep focusing on and telling yourself that narrative. If you believe you don't have enough time, well then Karen, I hate to tell you, you'll never have enough time. I'm sorry, Karen. Truly. It legit sucks to be a Karen these days. The point here is that our thoughts control how we see things; if we work at it, we can control the thoughts we allow ourselves to focus on.

Imagine what a difference it might make in your life if you started curating what you choose to focus on. What do you think might happen if you started focusing on telling yourself that you're worth respect and consideration? So, you eventually start getting better at setting boundaries with the different people in your life. It might be really uncomfortable at first, but one day, you realize that your life is suddenly so much more peaceful and that you're feeling more content.

It didn't happen overnight. It was because you started with choosing what you allow yourself to focus on every day. Instead of being Meredith Grey standing there batting her doey little eyes, asking McDreamy to "pick me," YOU pick YOU! A favorite quote of mine is currently my cover pic on Facebook, which states, *"There will come a time when you pick yourself, and that will be the beginning."*

When you start telling yourself that "I'm Possible," you become unstoppable. It doesn't happen overnight. You might not even believe it at first. You don't have to. Just print out the words and stick them up somewhere you will see them every day, like in your bathroom, bedroom, on the fridge, or wherever. Stick an "I am enough" temporary tattoo on you because maybe you have some commitment issues. Then, a "you are beautiful" sticker on your rearview mirror. "I am worthy" on your thumb ring. Whatever works for you! Eventually, those connections in your brain that previously followed a pathway that said *"I'm not worth it"* or *"I'm not capable"* start following a different route. The neurons in your brain start sending a different message to one another, and eventually, that old pathway falls away because you're not focusing on it anymore. You're saying "***Penelope***" to that asshole in your brain**.**

On that day, when you stop for a second and realize that you've made this change and you now feel like you're capable of sticking up for yourself and you finally believe in yourself - you go buy yourself a crystal pig with wings in a dome and put it somewhere that you can see it every day.

Because you are and have always been worth it.

Chapter 10

Pick Your Battles

I find it strange how we all have these remnants from childhood that dictate how we live our lives in adulthood, including our attachment styles, personality formation, emotional regulation skills (or lack thereof), level of self-worth, etc. Yet so few people ever teach their children how to do what we aren't able to do for ourselves. I guess it comes down to "you don't know what you don't know." I seriously think it should be part of our educational curriculum, though. Imagine a generation of adults who can practice emotional regulation. Just imagine, for a second, what kind of impact that would have on future generations.

I've become an advocate for others because I never had anyone who advocated for me. It's often the case with the healers and fixers in the world. When you don't feel seen as a child, you will do anything to be seen and receive the nurturing you crave so much. So, you become that person who gives all of themselves in hopes of being seen, validated, and loved. I mean, it beats the alternative of the child who makes national news for taking her parent's car for a joy ride at age 12, or the teenager arrested for shoplifting, or the kid who gets hooked on substances as a way to gain the attention they crave. But trust me, the people-pleasing version comes at a great personal cost as well!

My parents did their absolute best with the awareness and tools they had at the time, and I love them for who they are and for all they have given me. At some point, you need to stop looking back. What you need is to take a good, long, hard look at yourself and the role you play in your current relationships.

Are you allowing people to cross your boundaries and take advantage of you? Are you perpetuating certain toxic cycles? Are you practicing awareness in how you treat others and yourself on a daily basis? Are you paying attention to what's going on inside of you? Do you provide yourself with what you need or seek it outside of yourself?

As a natural advocate/fixer/healer, I've lost my identity to fight someone else's battles for them more times than I care to admit. There comes a point, though, where you must learn how to separate yourself from what is yours and what is not. You need to learn how to place your focus on fighting your own battles while allowing others to do the same. I have found that you only learn this as you get older. I think that when you get to your forties, you're just too tired of carrying other's shit for them, and once you put it down, you kinda realize that you never had to carry it in the first place. It's only then that you start working through your own shit that you've been neglecting all these years.

Apart from learning how to pick the battles I choose to fight, I've also learned how to *pick* my *passions*! These are the things and the people and the causes who fill my cup. *My cup* of life, Karen, not my cup of coffee or alcohol!! Then again, I guess I am pretty damn passionate about my coffee beans, grape juice, and fermented potato liquid! Here though I'm referring to the things and people that add true value to my life, my joy, and my peace. It's taught me that not everyone is supposed to be part of your life forever. Some people enter your life to teach you a lesson. Some are here for a season. Some for a few seasons. Some for a lifetime. When you accept this, you can let go of those relationships that might have left you with a scar or two without holding on to resentment or bitterness. Maybe they taught you how not to allow others to take advantage of you when they did just that. Maybe they taught you how to speak up for yourself when they pushed you down. Maybe they taught you to be more cautious about allowing someone's voice in your ear to so heavily influence your decisions and actions. So many of our trials and tribulations are there to teach us and help us grow as individuals. That's perhaps why we go through it. So we can *grow* through it. Just because you can do this doesn't mean you have to let them back into your life. I want to make that very clear. It means you don't deny them their need for sustenance, just not at your table. They can watch from the other side of the gate!

When you're a single parent, it can be challenging to gauge whether you're taking your own suffering out on your child or not. How many times have you had a tough day at work, only to come home and scold your child for causing a minor inconvenience? I'm not saying it makes you a bad parent. We're all human. I just find it challenging to balance being a disciplinarian and a parent at times. As a single mom with no partner in crime, I don't get to tap out when I'm struggling. There's no one to tag in when I'm about to lose my shit, so I try not to sweat the small stuff and save my energy for the big stuff. I have to check myself sometimes to ensure I'm not playing warden of the house because I'm on my own and may feel the need to overcompensate. On the flip side I also have to ensure I'm not avoiding necessary confrontation out of mom guilt from the divorce, a demanding job, and family struggles. I have to double-check myself to ensure I'm dealing with AJ based on AJ and not old trauma from past experiences. AJ is AJ and not, in fact, his dad or my brother or my mom, so I strive to make sure I remind myself of that if I'm triggered.

Then, there's learning how not to allow others to get to you—learning not to engage or respond to anything that's not worth your energy expenditure. Silence IS a response. Again, simple…NOT easy. Actually, it's hard! Some people know exactly which buttons to push, and then some folks just really need a glue stick instead of Chapstick. Or a throat punch. Or they're "keyboard Internet gangsters" whose fingers should be broken. Luckily for some, orange is not my color, so I don't fancy having to fight off big Betty as her new cellmate because she wants to make me her bitch. I'm no one's bitch, and you really don't want to test that boundary. I call bullshit on Orange is the New Black, and frankly, it washes me out a bit. So, to that snarky email chastising you that doesn't request any feedback or information from you in the end…delete! To that person who is relentlessly attacking via a text thread…block! To that "best friend" who not only didn't show up for you but chose to be critical and unsupportive at your lowest point…take care! Life is short and time is precious so use yours wisely and on the relationships with those who have your back, speak the truth even when it hurts, and are there to sit in the mud with you when that is where you need them!

Just remember, no response *IS* a response. And a very powerful one at that. Sometimes, it is more powerful than any other response you could give. Sometimes, the best response is no response at all. And with those who like to mob and involve all the family or all the friends, block them. Regain your peace and stand in your power. No one has the right to bully, berate, or insult others, and if they're a repeat offender, walking away is sometimes your only option for self-preservation. And sadly, as heartbreaking as it may be, those friends or family members who continue to simply sit idly by and watch the attacks with no attempt at intervention may have to be distanced from as well.

Especially when it comes to the energy vampires in your life, you know the type—those who are always complaining and draining your energy. The ones who are always seeking for you to provide them with validation, empathy, and understanding, yet they never add anything to your life. God forbid you share some of your own hardships just to get a "sucks to be you" type of response. Man, that really grates my cheese. That "friend" you share your sob story with that responds by saying, "I don't know what to tell you," and then goes no-contact during the hardest season of your life. To them, I say: "*So long, farewell, auf Wiedesehen, goodbye. Adieu, adieu, to yieu and yieu and yieu.*" Sing it with me now!

I could simmer down, but I like myself better, all feisty and shit. You won't. Trust me. This past year's favorite gift was a Christmas ornament that said, "Go ahead. Underestimate me. That will be fun!" What made it even more special is that it came from one of those high school band moms of another kid I mentioned in an earlier chapter that was essentially my stand-in parent at performances cheering me on! I'm 45 years old, and she's still one of my biggest supporters!

I've learned that all of this awareness only comes when you start focusing on healing yourself. It fixes your vision, and you start noticing things that weren't there before. But they were, and they might even have made you feel uncomfortable, but you could never pinpoint exactly what it was. That is until your self-worth grows and you start to see how some people have been disrespecting your boundaries and taking advantage of you for so long. You start noticing how some people are all about themselves, always taking but never giving. You see the insecurities and threatened tiny egos behind the passive-aggressive jokes.

"Oh, calm down, it was just a joke." "You're being too sensitive." "I didn't really mean you're a bitch, I was just joking." No, you weren't, and sending a smiley face or "ha-ha" over text to try and undo your real personality, having slipped out by accident, won't work.

People generally don't like change, and when you're doing the work to heal yourself, you undergo many changes. This might be scary for some onlookers because they're starting to realize they won't be able to walk over you or disrespect you without consequences. Where you may have remained silent previously, you're now starting to stand taller and speak up for yourself. You are beginning to understand the value of your voice, and some situations no longer deserve your time, energy, or focus.

BOUNDARIES! We've been doing it wrong all along. You see, many of us fear setting boundaries because we're worried about how the other person will react to us saying no. All the focus is on the other person, their needs, and their reaction. Screw that. Boundaries are about saying YES to your own damn self. Your needs. Your feelings, Your worth. You have to protect yourself because no one else can or will do it for you. Do you really want to keep taking the jabs disguised as jokes because you are afraid of their reaction if you speak up? Do you honestly want to live out the rest of your time here trying over and over again in hopes the person will change? Continuing to be there for others at such great personal cost when those same individuals refuse to stand up and say something to stop the verbal and emotional abuse? I assure you that sticking your head in the sand and pretending none of it is going on will not resolve a thing. I can promise you that pretending you don't hear the awful things being said or see the terribly hurtful things being done will NEVER lead to them not being said and done. To keep the peace? All this because of fear? Fear they will react poorly. Fear they will do something drastic. Fear it will backfire. For me, I broke and finally realized through a great deal of reading, writing, therapy, and yes Karen, coffee and alcohol, that I did not want to continue to pretend my heart and feelings didn't matter. I realized I didn't want to raise my son thinking this was normal and acceptable because it's family. I realized as I sat in the mud at the bottom of what the fuck lake that I couldn't do that anymore. For my sake and that of my son. I had to call it what it was and say it out loud. I had to pick me over them in order to save myself and AJ. It's been heartbreaking to see people fall away, but it has been eye opening also to see all those who have truly shown up. To have my self-respect back for taking a stand and saying no more. To tell that little girl inside me who so desperately wanted someone to stand up for me and have my back, "I got us". I've got me…oh so liberating!

Boundaries are hard, and especially so when they are completely foreign to us. I remember sitting with AJ and having a conversation about some changes in who was going to be around us and who wasn't. AJ responded by saying something like "I get it momma. I've seen it for a long time. Basically, we are punishing him for his behavior by not allowing him to see us". I sat back for a moment and explained to AJ that I had no desire to punish anyone and that my decision to establish a boundary was not to hurt anyone else, but rather protect us. That it was about ensuring our hearts and minds were safe from the chaos and hurt that came from that particular relationship. It was an emotional conversation for a momma and her 12yr old, but it also really helped me to see that my actions truly were about our well being and nothing else.

Merely setting boundaries is not enough, though. You need to follow through! The first step is always the hardest, but merely setting the boundary and then not doing anything when that person tests and oversteps the boundary makes your initial action null and void. The real challenge comes in the form of enforcing that boundary. We're all like children; we'll always push the boundaries, test the limits, and see what we can get away with. So, don't be surprised when others do it. We're all set in our ways, one way or another–and behavior change takes time and effort. If you want someone else to change how they behave around you, you need to give them some time and put in the effort by reminding them of how you want to be treated now, and not as before, so they can correct their behavior.

What if they don't? Or what if they disagree with your newly set boundary? Well, they don't need to agree with you in order to show respect. If someone cannot and will not adhere to the boundaries you set for them, then they don't deserve space at your table. Sorry. If your best friend came to you and told you that there's this person who keeps stepping over a boundary she set for him and asks you what she should do, what would you say? Tell him to hit the road, Jack, right? When the boundary is with family and they react negatively, do a deep dive. Ask yourself if this was someone outside of your family, what would they have to say if you shared it? Would your friends and family respond with fury that this had been said or done to you? Would they advise you to end that relationship as a result? If the answer to that is yes, then you have to wonder why they aren't responding in the same manner just because it's family?

A strong woman who is secure within herself, her identity, and her worth will never pull you down or overstep the boundaries you set for her. Period. That goes for any strong, mature individual. People who try to take advantage of you or pull you down do so because of their own insecurities. Some don't feel secure within their own abilities at work, so they make passive-aggressive jokes at work to try to a) break you down and b) get others to see you a certain way. It's got nothing to do with you and your abilities. It's all about them and their inabilities.

This is why you need to learn how to stand up for yourself, take up the space you so rightly deserve, and don't allow anyone to fuck with you. A friend of mine, all the way back in nursing school, told me that I needed to find my "bitch switch." I remember looking at her cluelessly, saying, "What's that?" She said the switch you flip that allows you to do what's best for you without feeling guilty about what other people may think or how they may react. Let's just say Noemi was about 20 years ahead of me in this healing quest. Bitch-switch it is! Because I matter! What AJ sees and is exposed to in family dynamics matters!

People won't like it. You'll get a lot of pushback. But just remember–Boss Bitches don't need to lie. In fact, they tell the truth behind your back and to your face. They have bigger balls than most men and more nerve than any Basic Bitch. If I pick a battle, I battle. Be ready. Because I am transparent to a fault, and I will call you out when others will not. It's sad, but I've realized that in business, hell, in the world, a woman who speaks the truth and doesn't just smile and nod and go along is a "bitch" or "emotional" or "too sensitive." When a man does the same, he's a savvy businessman or someone to be respected.

I have finally lived to an age where I can accept and protect my worth. So…go ahead. Call me a bitch. But make it, Boss Bitch, thank you very much!

Stop caring so much about what others think. Remember, lions don't lose sleep over the opinions of sheep. My motto: if it's not providing me with income, inspiration, love, or orgasms, it's not worth my time or attention.

Chapter 11

Approaching 40 - This Cannot be it!

Remember when we were kids, and we thought that people in their forties were old as fuck? You know, from back in the olden days. I feel bad for that now. Only because I now understand why some people in their forties might look old as fuck. Life is one scary ass roller coaster ride at times!

I spent several more years than I should have in my marriage. Mainly because I didn't want to face up to seeing myself as a "failure" and also because I didn't want AJ to have to go through the trauma of his parents getting a divorce. I felt no one else could love him like his father and I do. If I'm being completely honest, I was also afraid of what people would think. The judgmental whispers about me failing as a wife or the assumptions I was picking my career over my family. Fear of what my own family would think.

Nearing the end, we had gotten to where you barely grunt at one another. We'd try not to fight in front of AJ because we didn't want it to harm him. Kids pick up on these things, though. Parents sleeping in separate rooms. Sitting on separate couches. Living separate lives. There was a lot of built-up resentment and pain that we were both carrying. It wasn't until one morning when we were standing in the kitchen, his father on one side of the counter, myself at the other end, and AJ with his arms around us, trying to pull us in for a hug, saying, "AJ sandwich." When AJ was younger and our marriage wasn't circling the drain, we used to hug each other with AJ squished and squealing with laughter between us. It broke my heart that he remembered that and was physically trying to pull us back together. I realized then, in that moment, that our marriage was beyond saving, and it was hurting our son as well. It was time to end it.

Sometimes, your mind just needs a little more time to accept what your heart already knows. To me, I've lived by the motto of "*failure is not an option*" for so long that I just couldn't wrap my heart around a broken home for my son. Knowing something is over and ending it are two very different things. It took me well over a year and things getting pretty toxic and unhealthy for everyone involved to finally pull the trigger on what I knew in my heart for quite some time was the right thing. The dissolution of our marriage.

Unless you know what it's like to lose your own peace of mind, you'll never truly understand the significance or value of it. It took me forty years, losing it once and coming close to losing it a second time, to decide that I'll never allow that to happen again. If we're lucky enough, we learn the lessons set before us the first time. If not, you get a do-over and a whole lot of pain (that could've been prevented) until you finally learn the lesson. Sadly, many people never learn the lessons life presents them with and live a perpetual life of Groundhog Day—doomed to repeat the same relationship patterns over and over until the end of time. This is where that idea of "this is just my fate" becomes so crucial. It's not fate! It's our inner self using past experiences to subconsciously guide our decisions. And most of us don't even realize it. It takes a lot of work and self-examination to get a handle on that, but girl, that shit is eye-opening. If you can hang in there for the revelations and life-changing growth, you can turn those into a personal evolution!

I've seen too many couples try and stick it out "for the kids." Not realizing that their kids would be better off if they had two happy parents, albeit separated, rather than two miserable parents in an unhappy relationship. It took me longer than it should have to learn that lesson, but I am extremely grateful that the penny finally dropped on AJ sandwich day. Looking back, I think part of why it took me so long was because of what had been modeled to me as normal growing up. I have no doubt there were stretches, years even, where my parents stayed together because of us. We were all under one roof, but there wasn't joy or physical or emotional intimacy. It was more of an environment of co-existing with kids. It's scary what we can begin to believe is normal based on what we have experienced growing up.

Just because it doesn't work out doesn't mean either of us is a bad person. Sometimes, you just outgrow one another and the relationship. It's when we try to fit a square peg into a round hole for years on end that frustration and resentment build up—all the years of putting in the effort, emotions, and commitment, just to realize that it will never fit. You know what, it's okay if it doesn't fit. What's important is that you realize it and move on to find your square hole rather than allow yourself to be miserable your whole life. Not everything is meant to be forever.

It's now five years later, and we attended one of AJ's parent-teacher conferences together. This was big because we hadn't been around each other for more than five years. AJ whispered in my ear as we stood in line waiting to get started, "Well, this is awkward." I put on my big girl panties and did everything I could to prevent that from being the case. I made small talk and even made us all laugh a few times. As we approached the gymnasium, we both tried to fit through the door at the same time, shoulder-to-shoulder, causing me to slam my arm into the door. It caused an immediate goose egg and a nice scratch. Right then, it hit me again: square peg, round hole, and a lot of "forcing it." In the end, you always end up with a couple of bruises, scratches, and scars.

Our story was just one of being in completely different places in our lives. I'm the fixer, remember? I was also always the provider. With that, I've realized there comes a level of enabling if you don't realize that your providing allows your partner to sit back and not make an effort. It took me a long time to realize that you can provide the resources, opportunities, and support to someone, but you cannot provide the ambition, the work ethic, or the desire for self-improvement. How does the saying go? You can lead a horse to the water but can't make it drink. That was a really difficult and expensive lesson for me to learn. It's difficult because it's heartbreaking when you love that person, and all you want for them is to live a full, happy life. I put him through a few different programs for career advancement, but none worked out. I supported him in starting a handyman-type business and leaving his hospital job when some issues arose for him with that employer. I even surprised him with a trailer he wanted for those purposes.

A big-ass red bow on a big-ass flatbed trailer delivered by Santa Allie in the driveway in the middle of the night! I was buying tools and paying for gas, etc., for him to get going, but there was no money coming back in. I thought we'd build and grow together, but after eight years of dating and nearly ten years of marriage, I realized I was the only one building.

I don't care what anyone says. Whether you're a feminist, a womanist, or the opposite–existing as a woman in this world is hard. It just is. And I don't even mean that subjectively. I mean it factually.

A third of all women worldwide fall victim to sexual assault. One hundred fifty-three countries on this planet have laws in place that discriminate against women economically. Eighteen of those countries have made it legal for husbands to prevent their wives from working or pursuing a career. Less than twenty percent of the world's landowners are women. Two-thirds of illiterate people are made up of women. A large gender gap still remains in women's access to decision-making and leadership roles worldwide. Twelve million girls under the age of 18 are married each year to adult men. One woman or girl is killed every eleven minutes by someone in her own family. Women work longer hours while earning less money. Women in leadership positions earn 77 cents compared to every dollar for a man in the same position.

Not a single country on this planet has achieved gender equality.

We can't win, no matter which way we turn.

But you know what? There are so many women in countries you don't even have any knowledge of that are oppressed in ways you couldn't imagine. At least you and I have the freedom of choice, mostly. We can choose what to do with our lives. We can choose what to accept and what not to accept. Divorce isn't a tragedy. No one ever died of divorce. I learned through this experience that the tragedy is staying in an unhappy, unsupportive, unfulfilling marriage. Making each other miserable and teaching your children the wrong things about love and what it looks like. Divorce won't kill you. Domestic abuse might. Depression might. Rape might. Hunger might.

Women are not intended to be rehab centers for poorly raised men. It is NOT your job to fix him, change him, or raise him! You want a partner, not a project, and certainly also not a DICKtator.

Behind every strong, independent woman is a younger, broken version of herself who had to learn to pick herself up and never depend on anyone to rescue her.

A therapist once said to me: "*If you're not having sex, he may as well be your brother.*"

A sexless marriage is a friendship. Although it could potentially be a true partnership to a degree, without the intimacy, it isn't a long-term, fulfilling marriage for either party involved. I wanted counseling and for him to see a specialist, but that was a hard no for him until things had completely dissolved, and it was far too late for that. In his mind, it was all my fault because he'd "*never had an issue performing before me.*" Isn't it weird how people will blame anyone other than themselves when challenges or issues arise? After years of trying to save our marriage, I realized I had to leave that desire to save him and to save us behind for the reality of saving myself. Otherwise, I might not have made it out at all.

I take responsibility for the part I played. I moved a boy out of his mother's house and somehow expected a man to move into mine. I expected a decisive and supportive partner without him having any experience running a household, even if just for himself. I also realized that I married my best friend at the time, which in and of itself isn't a bad thing, right? But what I found was that although I loved him very much, I was never in love with him. I was naive and inexperienced and didn't know there was a tremendous difference between loving someone and being IN love with someone. I thought I could support him into a career, and once that failed, support him into being a successful business owner.

But I finally realized you can't motivate someone else to want more or do more for themselves. Motivation comes from within, and you cannot control anyone's actions but your own.

For my troubles, I had all the blame shoved onto me for being a strong, motivated woman. I was told by many, some in my own family even, that his passive-aggressive behavior of trying to sow a seed of resentment in my son towards me with chirps like "*Go ask the CEO*" was my fault. It was my fault because I emasculated him by paying all the bills, taking the responsibility of making all the decisions, and pushing him to be his best self. I remember telling my brother, who had been the "dude of honor" in our wedding, that I'd been asking for a separation for months. Counseling for years. I remember him saying, "Well, I hope you know what you're doing. There's no one decent left in El Paso, so you'll end up alone, and you're going to lose half of everything you have." I remember being flabbergasted and thinking, wow, okay, so stay in an unhappy, and at that point, incredibly unhealthy toxic marriage to keep my money and avoid singledom? I'm not going to lie; my divorce cost me a considerable amount of my hard-earned money and responsible financial management/planning, as well as everyone I'd considered and treated as my family on his side, but I bought my freedom. His entire family that I'd loved and treated as my own immediately dropped me and it was as though I'd never existed. But in the end, I bought my peace.

Don't let anyone tell you or convince you that your independence as a woman is the cause of your failed marriage or your singleness. Being a strong woman is NOT the cause of your loneliness, and being single does not automatically mean someone is lonely. You've chosen to be alone rather than be with someone who's never there for you while you continue to do it all yourself anyway. And buddy, let me tell you, once a woman has figured out she can do it all on her own, you'd better bring your A-game if you want in. Mediocrity just doesn't cut it anymore.

You can forgive someone and still not want anything to do with them! We all need to realize and remind ourselves that forgiveness is for past reconciliation, not for future consideration. Also, forgiveness is not so much about saying, "I accept what you did to me," or that it's okay. Forgiveness is about putting down the burden of pain you've been carrying as a result of what someone did to you so you can move forward without that burden dragging you down anymore.

Lao Tzu said it best when writing that new beginnings are often disguised as painful endings.

Sometimes, closure arrives years later. Long after you've stopped searching for it. You're just sitting somewhere laughing this laugh that is unapologetically yours. Mine is my obnoxious hack of a laugh that embarrasses me every time. As it trails off, the corners of my mouth hug my face, and it hits me, "I'm happy." I don't feel that anger inside of me anymore. Not bitterness. Not waiting for the other shoe to drop. Just happy. Just like that. With no fanfare or epiphany. Suddenly, you are grateful for any goodbyes that carried you to this moment. To the space you are now holding for yourself. It's a marvelous thing.

I realized I was "over it" when I no longer cared if people believed the lies about why we split. When it no longer bothered me that his entire family unfriended/blocked/threw me away. I did not need revenge. I realized that my no longer being his was punishment enough for him. I knew there'd never be another Allie in his life, and I realized the loss was truly his. Which, in itself, speaks to my having made the right choice for both myself and my son.

The game suddenly changed the moment I remembered who I was. It took me way too long to realize that if your partner is not your biggest fan, then you need to find a new partner. Or no partner at all. That's always an option. Please don't let society bullshit you into believing that you can't do life on your own, AND BE HAPPY DOING SO! I have, on and off for years now, and I love it. Yes, there are times when I feel lonely for intimacy. But I've also finally learned that there are different types of intimacy. We are duped into believing that intimacy only lives in romantic relationships. That's not true.

Intimacy is being able to bear (what you perceive as) the ugly parts of yourself to someone without fear of judgment. It's being able to show someone the birthmark on the butt that is your insecurities and not having to fear that they'll out you to the rest of the world. It's being able to just...be. Without pretense, without worry, without filters, etc. It's what grows from time spent together as you grow to care for one another and feel more comfortable in each other's company. This includes friends, coworkers, family, and, yes, romantic relationships.

Some people are once-in-a-lifetime. There is no upgrade after them. It took me four decades to realize that I am, in fact, a once-in-a-lifetime woman. That I am a catch despite my own insecurities and faults. The best gift my ex ever gave me was a new perspective on life. Before him, my biggest fear was being alone. After him, my biggest fear is settling or staying somewhere unhealthy and unhappy for far too long.

Sometimes, we cry because we feel like we've lost something. In this case, once I moved past the sadness, I started rejoicing in the knowledge that I had saved myself years of heartache by choosing my peace for a change. I didn't dread coming home from work on a three-day weekend anymore, wondering how I'd survive that. I got my peace back!

Marriage is hard. Divorce is hard. Choose your hard.

That being said, I was NOT prepared for the world of online dating in my forties–and man, has it been (yet another) learning curve.

Chapter 12

The Dumpster Fire of Online Dating

Being a strong, independent woman in this world is *hard*! It's a simple, cold, hard fact. We haven't quite evolved beyond the narrative of the working man and homemaking woman just yet. We've certainly come a long way, but we still have some way to go.

In my personal experience, most men haven't been taught to be secure enough to handle a strong, independent woman. They either feel intimidated by you, or they resent you. Or, worse yet, you get those who see an opportunity and jump on to ride the gravy train!

Sometime after my marriage ended, my friends started telling me I needed to "get back out there." To be honest, the idea of having to enter the dating scene again was really scary and intimidating. I mean, I hadn't been on a date in decades. I wasn't sure if it even worked the same way anymore. Note to self….it does NOT!

Nowadays, it's all about online dating. It makes "meeting" someone easier and more accessible. I mean seriously. Swipe left or right on another human being? Right at your fingertips. However, you never really know who you're talking to on the other end. Have you seen the series The Tinder Swindler on Netflix? How do you know who you're talking to is who they say they are? You don't. So, the thought of putting myself out there and being either catfished or ghosted or swindled or whatever else is scary shit.

Never mind the cumbersome process of having to spend all the hours, days, months, and years getting to know someone all over again if you *do* swipe right and things start to develop. The idea of telling my story over and over and over again in pursuit of a longstanding relationship.… utterly exhausting. At my age, this most likely entails having to get to know their children and navigating the issues surrounding not being their mother and them potentially not liking the new woman in their father's life. Then there's my son. Twelve going on 21, who is quite opinionated and thinks he should meet someone just to check them out *before* I go out with them! Huh? Who died and made you my keeper? However, recently, when I said I'd gotten a babysitter because I had a date, and he asked whether he had a car and whether or not he was employed, I almost spit out my coffee. I said, "Excuse me," to which he replied, "Well, someone needs to vet these people." He's soooo my kid!

Then, once I went out with him, AJ wanted to know his red flags. I said that we'd only been out once, and I didn't see anything glaring as of yet. I thought about it for a second, and at the risk of great personal harm, I asked AJ what he thought my red flags would be. You know. If a man I was dating were to ask him what my red flags were, what would he say? Now, I had a few ideas of what he might say, and honestly cringed as I awaited his response. But no. Instead, this brutally-honest-and-wise-beyond-his-years-tween of mine, said something that brought tears to my eyes. He didn't even hesitate to respond instantaneously with "me." I said what do you mean? He said, "Well, I'm your red flag. What man wants to date a chick with a kid?" My heart fell to the floor. Or even better, I'll steal a line from one of my favorite comedians, Kevin Hart, when he said, "*My belly button fell to my asshole.*" I told AJ that any man who thought my AJ was a red flag could fuck all the way off to the top of fuck off mountain and then just keep right on going.

Don't even get me started on the awkwardness of the meeting of the families and everyone trying to navigate this weird new situation they need to try and at least seem supportive of. Or you date the guy whose red flag pops up when you've been dating several months, and he's talked all about the Christmas Eve gathering he's hosting at his house and doesn't include you. I mean the menu of what he's serving and who all is going and that he'll have the game on for people to watch in one room and music in the other type of level of detail and then nothing. No invite. No conversation about why perhaps the meeting of the family/friends should be held for now. Literally nothing. So are you married and not telling me? Are there bodies in the basement or heads in the freezer or something? Am I not the right color or size or age or what?

I find myself looking at all of the effort it takes and thinking to myself, "Is it really worth it? Is this really something I want right now? I don't know." It's a lot.

Here's your public service announcement for today. You know those memes floating around with a picture of a dumpster on fire with writing that says, "Dating in your 40s is picking the least charred, unrecognizable flaming object out of the dumpster?" TRUTH! Man, it is slim pickings out there. I don't mean to sound like I'm a picky bitch, but seriously people. Is this really it? The check comes, and it just sits there. I don't mean to sound judgy, but multiple marriages with multiple women with multiple kids from said multiple marriages with multiple women!? Dinner with a wrinkled t-shirt with a hole in it and flip-flops. Endless "I don't know" answers. Where do you want to go? "I don't know." Where do YOU want to go? Ugh! I died laughing when a precious friend navigating a lot of this same stuff asked if the guys I've met have all their teeth and limbs. I'll leave those stories to your imagination as they're not mine to tell, but for real, what in the actual fuck!

In one of my favorite Seinfeld episodes, Elaine declares that 95% of men are undateable. To which Seinfeld replies, "UNDATEABLE!!" while gesturing with his hands dramatically. Elaine then asks, "*how the hell are all these people out there getting together*?" And Seinfeld says, "*Alcohol!*" That's a pretty accurate skit. However, it's more like "alcohol! An awful lot of alcohol!"

At some point, if you're lucky, you get to realize that doing life on your own and being lonely are two very different things. Just because you're single and living alone doesn't necessarily mean you're lonely. Yes, we are designed for connection, but not everyone is the same, and if it comes to having to choose between being in a crappy relationship or being on my own, I will choose to be on my own every day and twice on Sundays! Being brave enough to do life on your own as a woman frees you up to invite who you want into your life, not because you need them, but because you want them in your life. Most men can't deal with that. They need you to need them in order for them to feel secure within their own manhood.

Sorry, bud, that's not my job nor my responsibility. Don't get me wrong, having a manly man who knows his way around my parts AND the parts of my car and house that need attention would be amazing! But not at the cost of happiness. Not at the cost of my peace. Not at the cost of my self-respect. ***Never again!***

People constantly told me that I "need to get back out there," to which I'd respond, "Nah, I'm good, thanks." So many people just cannot fathom having to spend time on their own. The serial cheaters have to have the next one lined up and active before they leave the one they're with. The people who kick their friends to the curb when they meet the next Mr. Right, no matter how Mr. Wrong everyone tries to tell her he is. I never realized just how few people are comfortable in their own company, facing their thoughts and inner chatter. So then they'd tell me it's because I'm afraid to love again. It wasn't love that I was afraid of. I'm afraid of the possibility of the next guy being the same as the last one whose failures all but destroyed me. I'm just not willing to go there again. I don't know if I'd survive it.

Relationships are hard enough as it is. I already captain the ship at my workplace all day, every day. I don't want to have to do the same at home. I'm CEO at work and have no desire to be such in my personal life. I want to come home and take off my shoes, throw my bra in the hamper and be someone's partner. Not their mother or their boss. In my previous relationship and other relationships like at work or in friendships, I've realized that there are an inordinate amount of men who just cannot handle a strong woman. Moving forward, in order for him to date me, he needs to have a steady income and a functioning penis. Those are non-negotiable.

My new philosophy is that "*If they can't handle the sass, they can't have the ass.*" They wouldn't be able to handle it anyway! And let me tell you, with menopause here or approaching it has unfortunately become quite the ass. I think every calorie I consume now goes straight to my hips, thighs, and butt. I never had a butt! At all! So, imagine my surprise when the other day I came into the living room and AJ said "momma, turn to the side". I obliged as he has always been quite the wardrobe critic regarding my clothing choices and was stunned when he said "gyatt (look it up as I had to) you've got hips and a butt!" Oh my God this child of mine! No Brazilian butt lift here. Just a bunch of unbalanced hormones and a few too many "I'll just have a bite"!

Who knew it would be so hard to find a mature man who is respectable and knows how to treat a woman? First, you need to sift through those who make you pay for their dinner or don't ever text you back. Those who not only don't open your door or pull out your chair, but actually get out of the vehicle and go into the restaurant without you! True story! How about those who are caught up on their exes or have some perverted sexual preferences. Let me save you some trouble. I can now tell you that an upside-down pineapple is indicative of a swinger, and I'm not talking about the kind you'd find on a playground Karen! Ummmmm, NO?! Then there are those who don't know how to practice good hygiene, including regular dental care, and those who are all talk but can't get the soldier to salute when the time comes. Who knew that asking for a decent, normal guy with morals and a functioning penis is just too much. I mean, I'm perfectly okay with a guy needing to pop a little blue pill if he needs to but take care of it on your end. Don't feel embarrassed, and then try to make me out to be the cause of your non-functioning flaccid member. Also, don't tell me, "Oh, it is what it is." We're in our 40's for God's sake, not our 90's and I don't know about you, but I still have needs and urges in that department!

I'm not some sex-crazed freak. But as we established earlier, a relationship without sex is like being with your brother. Yes, there are different forms of intimacy, but I know what I want in my life. If you're okay with not having any, fine. You do you, Karen. I just know that I'm not happy with a non-sexual relationship anymore. I have needs, too, and if you can't fulfill them as my partner, as I would do yours, then it's just not going to work.

I was actually asked on one date whether I had an income requirement. Huh?! So, then I started saying that I'm a nurse whenever the question came up about what I do for a living. It's not a lie. I am a nurse. But then what do you do when it gets more serious and you suddenly have to explain that on top of being a nurse, you're actually also a hospital CEO who's responsible for an entire market? Or worse yet, they send you a pic of your pic from the hospital lobby saying how come you didn't tell me you ran the place? Oops. True story.

It's tricky because divulging that kind of information upfront can go one of a few different ways. Either he'll think that he's hit the jackpot and can start planning his retirement. He'll feel intimidated and will always try to one-up you to protect his fragile ego. He'll feel threatened and run away. He'll feel like he needs to "show you your place" and treat you like crap. Or perhaps he'll see the dollar signs and do whatever he can to get in, but then slowly lower the bar to the point where he sits around all day playing video games and golfing, running up your tab at the country club while you're out working your ass off to pay the bills.

Lastly, there's the ever-elusive unicorn of a man who can accept you for who you are. He is the kind of man who is secure within himself and will clap for you along the way just as you would for him. I was once given a fridge magnet that said if I were meant to be controlled, I'd have come with a remote! Clearly, I did NOT! I need a unicorn of a man who will support me in the way of allowing me to do my thing and say, "*That's my girl.*"

As women, we glow differently when loved and treated right. There are strong, independent women who still need tenderness, forehead kisses, and "arm time," as I call it. Meaning that I just want to curl up in his arms and take one of those deep breaths where it feels like nothing on Earth can hurt me, that all is right in the world, and that I am protected and cherished by someone I love. I want to feel that he's "got me." No matter what happens, he's got my back.

Women will be as girly as you pamper them to be. As submissive as your strength, support, and love allow. As intelligent as your security and challenging feeds and as sensually feminine as her lover entices.

I *WANT* to be the girl in the relationship. I've had to wear the pants in a relationship before, and I'd rather do life alone than be forced to do that again. I want a partner in every sense of the word! Emotionally, financially, sexually, mentally, and physically. ALL OF IT! Otherwise, it's just not worth the expensive investment for me anymore. And trust me, it is a very expensive investment. The kind that can wreck your life when lost*!* Emotionally, financially, sexually, mentally, and physically. ALL OF IT!

It's not worth the vulnerability needed to build something truly special and lasting if that person doesn't have what it takes to be a true partner who is dedicated to living up to their responsibilities within the partnership. Because on my side, I plan to live up to those responsibilities and expectations for a healthy, happy, long-term relationship. When you get hurt or sick - I've got you! Should you get laid off - I've got you. If you find yourself struggling in some way emotionally - I've got you! So, I need someone that's "got me" too! Otherwise….I DON'T have you!

I don't mean to sound like I think I'm the cat's whiskers or that my shit doesn't stink. I'm a self-declared hot mess express, after all. But I own my mess. This is about wanting to have a partner who will meet me halfway on every level. There's no 50/50. I give a 100%, and so does he. It's about finding someone who will give 190% on the days when I only have 10% to give and can barely get out of bed to brush my teeth. A man who is comfortable and secure enough to allow me to do the same for him when he needs it. Does that even exist anymore? Am I chasing fairytales? I don't know. What I do know is that if I end up not finding it, I'm more than happy to continue enjoying life *all* by myself.

My mother and my aunt repeatedly told me not to settle. I didn't listen. Get a prenup, at least, they said. I didn't listen to that advice either. I remember my divorce settlement; I told my divorce attorney, "*I'll never do this again. It hurts too much, and it's way too damn expensive.*" To which she replied, "*Yeah, you will.*" "You're young, and smart, and beautiful. You'll meet someone else. You just won't do it again without me!" That bit of advice I will heed! But I guess first, I'll need to swipe right, right?

It's five years later, and I'm not convinced that I'll ever marry again. You know what they say, "*never say never.*" However, I'm not even sure I even want to live with someone again.

You have to do what works for you, right? I recently read an article about a couple who got married and lived their life the way that worked for them. They have a double-story house. He lives upstairs, and she lives downstairs. They don't even spend every day together. He's a writer, she's a painter. They love one another but also enjoy their own company. It might seem weird to many people who are brought up to hold on to traditional ways of being in a marriage. But they're happy! Happier than most other married couples. So, who's to say what's right for another couple? I remember watching an interview a long time ago, and they asked Katherine Zeta Jones what the secret to her long-standing marriage to Michael Douglas was. Her answer? Separate bathrooms and separate closets. Brilliant!

One of the valuable lessons my failed marriage did teach me is not to settle ever again! Please understand that this is not a dig at my ex-husband, or anyone else from my past. By settling, I don't mean anyone is lesser than me. I mean, I desire someone who checks all my boxes. No one is perfect, and I'm far from it, but if I'm investing the finite amount of time, energy, and resources I have into another relationship, it will be with someone I not only love but am deeply in love with. I want it all, or I'm just fine all by myself. Well, not totally by myself. I still have my mini me in AJ, my fur babies, battery-operated lovers, and my friends! Experiencing a bit of loneliness here and there is nothing compared to a lifetime of loneliness in the wrong relationship. Like the late and wonderfully talented Robin Williams once said: "I used to think that the worst thing in life was to end up alone. It's not. The worst thing in life is to end up with people who make you feel alone." Ouch.

I remember my dad telling me after my breakup with fiancé number two that there is a big difference between being alone and being lonely. I realized I was lonely AND alone in my marriage. You can be just as alone in a relationship with the wrong person as you are when single.

The moment you settle for less than you deserve, you get less than what you settled for.

It took me a long time to learn that not every relationship lasts forever or has a fairytale ending. Not every person for whom we have deep feelings and who makes a home for themselves in our hearts is meant to stay there forever. Sometimes, people come into our lives to teach us what love is, and other times, to teach us what love is not. Some of the hardest lessons some people will leave you with are what not to settle for and how not to shrink yourself down to almost nothing ever again. How to ask for what you want, and how not to tolerate bullshit anymore. How to take up space, and how to live unapologetically. Some will up and leave and take a piece of you with them, but the lessons will always remain.

Here are five tips for women on what to look for in a man. Reading over it again almost makes me laugh, a discouraging kind of laugh to think that I might never find all of these qualities in a single man.

1. It is important that a man helps you around the house and has a job.

2. It is important that a man makes you laugh.

3. It is important to find a man you can count on and doesn't lie to you.

4. It is important that a man loves you and spoils you.

5. It is important that these Four men don't know one another.

You see, I believe that a princess sits and waits for her prince charming to come and rescue her, whereas a QUEEN will get off her ass and do it her damn self!

I'm not perfect, and I'm not looking for perfection in a partner. I'm looking for perfect for me and vice versa. There have been a few Mr. Right Now's over the years, but Mr. Right has mostly managed to escape my radar. I'm not looking for Mr. Perfect; I just know I deserve better than Mr. Wrong, that's for sure. I am strong, smart, and fiercely independent, and I'll never apologize for that ever again in my life. I am proud of who I have become and will not settle for anything less than what I deserve. I have high standards, and so far, no one has been able to meet them long term. Hence, the ex-husband and a growing list of Seinfeld's *undateables,* even with alcohol. I've had to figure out "me" before I could even think of a "we." That takes time, and I am continually working on myself so I can be the best version of me for myself, my son, and a potential future partner. I love having the freedom to do whatever I want, when I want, and how I want. It's addicting. Man Cave? Nah! I'll take the whole damn castle!

Hear me when I say that you need to stop giving discounts. Stop enabling the kind of toxic behavior in others that tears your heart into little pieces. Have the strength and respect yourself enough to walk away from anyone and anything that doesn't serve you anymore, help you grow, or no longer brings you joy. Check your price tag if you aren't treated with love and respect! Maybe you'll find that you've discounted yourself. Only

YOU can set your price. Only YOU can teach others how you want to be treated. Only YOU can teach others what's acceptable to you and what isn't. Get your ass off the clearance rack and back into the locked-up glass case where only the most valuable stock is kept. Because you are valuable. You are one-of-a-kind! There is no clearance sale here, honey.

I don't know about you, but I don't want someone standing beside me just because they're lonely, and I can provide them with a certain lifestyle. I want someone standing next to me because they can't imagine themselves standing next to anyone else, and vice versa. I want someone who will stand in front of me as a shield to protect me when I need it. Someone who will stand behind me when I'm doing my thing and shining or when I need them to have my back. I want someone who will pick me up and carry me when I'm not strong enough to do it for myself. I want all of these things because I know that I will give all these things and more to someone when I'm committed.

I'm humble enough to know that I'm replaceable but finally self-aware enough to know that it'll be a downgrade.

They say, "Someday, someone will walk into your life, and you'll finally realize why it never worked with anyone else." I honestly hope that is true, and I do hope it will happen for me. I would love nothing more than to have someone to share this life with. To make memories and laugh with. To love and to be loved by. However, if it's not in the cards, that's okay, too. I have made it through every challenge and struggle in my life thus far and will continue to do so. I'm finally in a place where I know I'll pick myself above becoming something I'm not just to make someone else feel more comfortable. Fuck that.

The illustrious Meryl Streep recently said in an interview that women are fluent in speaking the language of men. We are taught how to speak men from childhood. The problem is that many or perhaps most men have never bothered to learn how to speak the language of women. I love that, and I think maybe it's time.

It took me a long time and a lot of heartache to finally conclude that I do not want to be someone's "sometimes." If what you're looking for is a booty call, power to you. There's no judgment here. For those of us a little more sheepish, with today's technology and discreet delivery available, getting your own groove on has become a whole lot easier as well! We all have needs. Even if we women tend to be judged very differently for our own needs. It's kind of despicable that in this day and age, men are still applauded for sleeping with multiple women and being the "stud" who keeps his options open while he "taps that." Women, on the other hand, will be called a slut faster than you can say, multiple men. Dating around? What a whore. Fuck off, Kevin!

What shifted my perspective was a meme I saw that said, "*You are not a life raft, you are not a compass, you are not breadcrumbs, you are not a flashlight, you are not a Band-Aid, and you are not a stop along the way as any man attempts to find himself. You are a destination. A whole, complete person who deserves another whole, complete person.*" Not a man that says to teach him how to love. Not a man who responds with that's just who I am, it's in my DNA when you share that something he does or says is hurtful to you. You are wonderfully and beautifully enough, just as you are. Maybe too enough for someone who cannot see your value. Too enough to be someone's "something" or "sometimes." You are EVERYTHING! Hence, the ring on my thumb that says, "*You are enough.*" Or my newest addition that I pull out on the really tough days that says: "*Remember who the fuck you are.*"

Being a strong, independent woman doesn't mean you don't need a man. It means that you need someone of equal value. Someone who won't be intimidated by your light, abilities, achievements, and strength. Someone in whom we can glow, grow, and conquer together.

Getting back onto the dating scene has been an eye-opening experience for me. It can be emotionally exhausting and downright mortifying at times. Shocking, even. However, it has brought with it some life lessons and friends that I know will last my lifetime, and if I'm being honest, some really funny shit too.

When I finally decided to give the dating thing another try, I went all Allie on it and threw myself into the experience. I don't do half-*ass*, remember? At the risk of sounding like a floozy, my girlfriends started teasing me at one point, saying that they needed to create a spreadsheet of my dating to keep up with my escapades. It sounds way worse than it actually is. A spreadsheet of men? Ha! More like a documentation of adventure! Being newly single after so many years with the same man, I figured I needed to browse and see what's out there. I also needed some practice getting back into this whole dating thing because, you know, it's been a while. It's been more than a while. It's been for fucking ever!

This idea of having my choices tracked opened my eyes to trends I may not have identified before. Which eventually led to the whole list of non-negotiables like:

- Must have a car.

- Must have a job of his own and be able to sustain himself.

- Must not live with his mother (unless she's elderly and in need of care, of course.)

- Must not be an alcoholic.

- Must not be a potential serial killer. Bodies in the basement are a hard no for me.

- Serial killers might be considered if they have a working penis and are gainfully employed.

- Kidding, or maybe not!

I don't have time for and do not want to teach a grown-ass man how to treat and love a woman. This isn't a "build-a-bae" store. This is real life. I've got things to do, places to go. I don't have time for bullshit. Been there done that once before. Then, a few times more because, apparently, once isn't enough for me to learn the lesson.

I assure you I'm not a slut, and to borrow Bill Clinton's famous line, "*I did not have sexual relations with all of these men.*" Okay, maybe I tweaked it a bit, but you get the gist. And I'm not lying as he did! And if I did, who the fuck cares. My life, my business. But I didn't. Some just made one date, some a few, others I ran from as fast as I could, and some are still in my life in some capacity. It's been an adventure of a journey, getting back on the horse. I've learned a lot about myself and others, and I continue to just enjoy the journey. They've all been given nicknames, you know, so my girlfriends can keep them straight and also to protect their egos.

Allie's Spreadsheet of Men

"Greece"

The timing has just never been right with this one. Work or family stuff kept getting in the way. Initially, we were both married, and then suddenly, we weren't. We both care deeply for one another, or at least I do. I know he says he does as well, but anytime there has been an opportunity for us to move forward, it passes us by without anyone having done anything about it. I'll come on strong, and he'll tease me for having what he calls "keyboard courage." Every time I've worked up the nerve to actually back it up with an invitation, he'd disappear faster than my tween when it's time for chores. However, I must give credit where credit is due. He deserves recognition for his significant contributions in regard to the Allie I am today. Our friendship has allowed me to see myself through the eyes of another. To truly recognize what I bring to the table and to believe in myself and my talents. When I shared with him that I was going to write a book, he was extremely supportive. When I've talked about wanting to start my own consulting business, he's said repeatedly, "what are you waiting for". His unwavering belief in me helped me develop that belief in myself.

Is he actually just full of shit or blowing smoke? Is he maybe afraid of the outcome, commitment, or failure perhaps? Who knows. I don't know that I'll ever know. I'm not sure I want to know. Maybe the idea of what it could be keeps us both engaged, when in all reality we'd probably kill each other. The fantasy of what we wish it to be. Sometimes, fantasy is far better than the actual thing. In this case, I may never know, but I think I may always want to.

"El Puto Grande"

I'd just started out on the dating apps and this guy reaches out. He's an attorney. Divorced with two young girls. We've been chatting for a week or so and he says he's on a ski trip but wants to meet me in person as soon as he gets back. We make some tentative plans and I go on about my day. I've convinced a few of my girlfriends to join a mimosa crawl being held in downtown El Paso. We sit down at the 1st stop and are catching up. I tell them about this new prospect and of course they demand to see his picture and profile. Imagine my surprise when my sweet friend says, "what the fuck?" My attorney prospect is her ex-husband! A drug and drink addicted real piece of work who told me he's on a ski trip and told her he's out of town on business so he couldn't take their girls for yet another of his weekends! I was dumbfounded. You'd think that one occurrence would've been enough for me to quit online dating, but no! Have you not been listening? Me? I NEVER learn a lesson the 1st time or the easy way. I keep going until I get that proverbial bonk on the head. So…. next!

"Jake from State Farm, a.k.a. Angry Eyes"

I'm a bit of an adrenaline junkie, so with date #1 being an invitation to go jeep crawling, I was sold! You never know what you're in for these days, so I shared my location with a friend just in case I went missing so they'd know where to look for my body. Fun fact…when your friend and her mother share a name, make sure you're texting your active location for your date to the right one! The messages started flying asking if she and her husband should come right away when I inadvertently texted Mama T. "Should we call 911?" With a giant emoji waving a red flag. Oops. Imagine my horror when I realized I'd sent my location to my friend's mom instead. Hilarious and another sign of the times.

It started off great with a campfire in the desert mountains, wine, and a picnic dinner! Unfortunately, it went downhill from there. The few dates we went on helped me realize that I don't have to worry about being an alcoholic. I always think people might think me an alcoholic because I joke about drinking as a coping mechanism for stress at work. I make comments such as tequila is cheaper than therapy. It's just that though, a joke. Well, kinda. I may or may not be a member of half the wineries in Fredericksburg, and I have a crazy dream of opening a winery geared toward healthcare folks like myself. You know, open 24 hours for the night crew to enjoy and staffed by folks full of dark humor with a mascot therapy dog that everyone can love on.

This guy, though! He'd bring three bottles of wine on our date. I'd have two glasses, and he'd polish off the rest. And he'd still be fine! Yikes! I know what alcoholism can do to a family. I've seen it plenty of times as a nurse. And then he tried to sell me insurance, hence the nickname!! No, thank you! Next!

"The Medic"

We've both been there for one another when we've needed it, but when the need passes, so do we. Repeatedly. He once gave me a card about hope being the light within. Said something about the goodness *within* me, bringing out the goodness in those around me. About how that was how bright my light shines and how strong I am.

He bought me a "full of lipstick courage" canvas as a reminder that all I need is a bit of red lipstick, and I've got this that hangs in my office to this day!

"If you're sad, add more lipstick and attack."
- Coco Chanel.

"Sprouts"

A chef, you say? In my age bracket, you say? Not bad looking, you say? Just hold up a minute. This could be something. We'd been chatting it up on match.com for several weeks, and it had been going really well.

He brought up the idea of potentially meeting up for a date but shared that he was unable to drive due to a DUI (driving under the influence) charge. Umm, red flag much? Abort mission!

Well, not me. I mean, we all make mistakes, right? Let's not jump to any conclusions. Poor guy probably just had one too many and is paying the price. But then, I'm walking through Sprouts doing some grocery shopping one day, and "the chef" is working behind the deli counter. I had to do a double take and thought to myself, "No, it can't be." But just then, I heard someone ring the deli assistance button and call out his name. I bolted and never spoke to him again.

No, Karen, it's not because I'm some rich bitch who thinks that she's too good for the deli-counter guy. It's because he had already been lying to me. He's not a chef. I don't care that he works behind a deli counter. Get over your own insecurities and just be honest about who you are right now. An aspiring chef? Awesome! A washed-up chef with a drug problem, a string of DUI's and a liar? No thank you!

Have you ever wished that, just once, a liar's pants would actually catch on fire? Or their nose would start growing as they're spewing their bullshit?

I like to think that I was saved by the bell. The deli bell!

"Great balls of fire"

A fireman, you say? Like one of those in the yellow-orange getup with the giant hose running into danger to rescue people instead of running away with everyone else? Yes, please! True story…I agreed to do an elementary school fundraising run (or walk), so I signed up at AJ's request. It's an annual tradition at his elementary school. They'd block off a mile of the street behind the school, and entrants ran at the sound of the gun with their children to the finish line. Remember, we've already established that I don't run unless something is chasing me. Picture this (in my best Sophia voice from the Golden Girls.) It's downtown El Paso, 2018. Imagine my horror when AJ and I are standing at the starting line chatting and waiting for things to get started, and I hear someone from a distance yell, "Allie?" I'm looking around and don't see anyone, figuring it's one of the other couple hundred folks there. But no, there it is again. God? Is that you? NOPE! AJ excitedly points out it's the fireman at the top of the ladder. AJ's all excited because the cool fireman 100 feet in the air knows his mama. Me? I'm more like, "Oh fuck me." Now I MUST run. I can't let this dude see me walking the wild cat mile! So run I did. Until my legs were jello, and I was coughing so hard, I thought I might vomit. So yeah, three blocks in, and I'm doing a walk of shame. Okay, it may have been like ¾ mile, but still, I could've died. With his crazy fire department and custody schedule combined with the insanity that is my calendar, we just seemed to never be able to make it work to connect.

"Momma's Boy"

The first date was going really well until he casually dropped by saying that he'd like to invite me over for dinner so I could meet his mother. Initially, the alarm bells went off, and I thought, *"Uhm, this is a little fast, to say the least. He must really like me?"* Then it became clear that for me to visit him at his home meant I'd have to meet his mother because he lives with her. As in, always has, and likely always will. Dude. And now that I think of it, there are a couple others that are going to think this one is about them if they read this. Seems to be a bit of a theme these days.

"The Counselor"

Love bomb alert! On date number two, he introduced me as his girlfriend and said he loved me. Run, you say? But why? It feels so good when someone pulls out of your driveway, hanging halfway out of their truck window, shouting: *"I will change your mind about marriage and marry you one day, Allie Trimble."* It's the stuff of fairytales. Who wouldn't want that? It felt magical.

But, alas, it sadly didn't last. It was, in fact, just a love bomb. At the three-month mark, I saw it for what it was and walked away. I never heard from him again.

"Hola, or Cocktail Pic Dude"

This one may sound vaguely familiar, as I mentioned him in the chapter about using your words. Here's the longer version as to why. Our very first date was a double date with a couple who set us up because they thought we'd make a good match. They thought because he supposedly likes strong, powerful women with a bootie (remember menopause and my all natural BBL), and I liked intelligent men who made an honest living and had their shit together, we'd be a match. It was fun, and at least the idea of us was great. I mean a retired firefighter finishing up a degree in architecture who is extremely handy around the house and at least appears to be one heck of a dad?? Winner winner chicken dinner! Our second date was dinner and drinks soon after the first, and we both had a great time. Then, I started receiving random messages of a picture of a cocktail he'd be drinking along with a "hola." Or just a "hola." Then, he sends me that song by Rob Base and DJ E-Z Rock, "It takes two to make a thing go right." Initially, I was like, "I love that song!" I missed his intended message. It hit me soon after, though. He was trying to tell me that he feels like he's putting in all the effort and wants me to make more of an effort because it takes two to make something like this work.

In a song! He sent me a song to communicate this. USE YOUR WORDS, for fuck's sake. How am I supposed to devise that you're trying to tell me something? Luckily, I'm blonde but not stupid, so I eventually caught on, even though it took me a moment.

I shared with him that I have no desire to do the chasing in the relationship. That I'd had to play the role of the one who "wears the pants" before and just won't go there again. He said that he didn't need that but that some reciprocity would be nice. Now keep in mind, all this after two dates!?

The last time he sent me a pic, calm down, Karen. It wasn't a dick pic. No, he sent another picture of a cocktail he was merrily sipping on. I replied, saying that it looked nice. He invited me to join him. I couldn't, as I had AJ at the time. And that was that. I did, however, get a "Merry Christmas Allie" several months later and then a "Happy New Year Allie" text message from the guy. You snooze, you lose. And it was kinda funny because he shares his name with my son's elf on a shelf, so it may have been difficult to take him seriously long-term anyway!

Thinking back now, I'm okay with that. After all, the egg doesn't swim to the sperm. Never do the pursuing or the chasing ladies! It just leads to you having to wear the pants and do everything on your own in the long run. Unless you're gay, then one of you kind of has to do it. I've often wondered if that might just be easier. I have several gay friends that I absolutely adore, but as I've already said, the whole working penis thing is a deal breaker for me.

"Coach"

A basketball coach who is a bit of a legend in our town, taught me to never apologize for being a strong, independent woman. Yes, I needed someone to teach me that, just like we all need reminding or teaching sometimes. He gave me grace and a second chance after I ran for the hills out of fear a few years before.

My peace came with his encouragement to live and thrive where my feet are today. To not ruminate and stress over where they've been or worry and have anxiety over where they're going. Just focus on where they are right now. "Focus on where your feet are." I like that. It's a nice little mindfulness reminder.

He's soulful and a coach through and through, meaning he's *ALWAYS* encouraging and motivating others to strive for bigger and better and to never settle for less. It makes me sad to think how much of himself he dedicates to the growth of others and yet can't quite find a way to encourage himself. He's not been dealt the easiest hand in life and has his own share of demons to deal with. This was a hard one to walk away from because he's a wonderful man in his soul. I really care about him. But his difficulty in facing and fighting for better days for himself as opposed to just sitting and wallowing in the struggles he has is emotionally draining and something I do not have the capacity for. I'd say something with nothing but good intentions, and it would cause a big problem after it was perceived and interpreted differently than I intended. The ability to regulate our own emotions is a must. If people are easily triggered and unwilling or unable to see the earnestness in your support or commentary, it's a non-starter. I know we see his potential & see that he needs to be loved & healed, but understand this: a man like that won't be able to fully love you back the way you deserve. He may really love you, but he won't know *how* to love you. This relationship will DRAIN the SHIT out of you.

In the end, there will always be positive vibes and well wishes between us, and I have the utmost respect for him as a coach, as a father, and as a man.

This situation reminded me of a lesson I thought I'd already learned: We can't save everyone, and certainly not when their number one priority isn't to save themselves. No matter how desperately we may want to!

"Royal Flush"

This one is complicated and has come around more than once. He has taught me what it's like to receive the kind of care and spoils I have always given to others. He has taught me to receive love and support from someone in a way I've never been the recipient of, only the bestower. No strings attached kindness and generosity. Nothing thrown in your face or held over your head when things sour. I couldn't figure out why I hadn't walked away when there were so many little things telling me to leave the first time around. Once I did finally walk away, however, I realized that I've never had someone look after me like I do for others. Just for me. Without any expectations of something in return. Small things here and there. Weekend getaways. He'd tell me to only worry about AJ and work, and he'd take care of everything else. I'd never had that before. Ever!

We took over a year apart. Completely apart as in no contact, both dating other people, moved on kind of apart. Then, when unbeknownst to him I perhaps needed him most, we came full circle and have become closer than ever. I realized that a big part of our past struggles were mine to own. Yes, he can be a lot. Yes, he can drive me nuts at times. Yes, he is stubborn and super alpha and never wrong. Yes, he is a 40 something year old man who still essentially lives as a bachelor after never being married and having no children of his own. I tease him that I can trace his steps through the house by the trail of mess he leaves behind. But after a lot of self-work, I realized it was my own degraded sense of self-worth our first time around that had me constantly waiting for the other shoe to drop. Why would someone be this good to me? Why would someone do such nice things for me? When is he going to throw it in my face? When will I hear those stinging words of "but look at all I've done for you". Was he this good to AJ simply as a way to win me over? Was he stooping so low as to use my only child to secure his place with me? I couldn't enjoy being loved and spoiled for the 1st time in my life because I was too busy trying to figure out his ulterior motives. After a lot of self-examination and hard work on me, I came to realize the 2nd time around that he simply loves me. Loves AJ. And because of that love and care he WANTS to do nice things for us. Who knew? I am extremely grateful for him. He granted me the gift of being able to experience what it feels like to be spoiled the way I always spoil the people I love. He helped me realize that it's not selfish to set and enforce boundaries with friends, family, and anyone else who doesn't treat me the way I want and deserve to be treated. He is my biggest supporter and my #1 fan, as well as that of AJ. He and AJ are frighteningly similar in many ways and have become two peas in a pod. He is incredibly good to me as well as AJ, and we will see what develops over time. Living where my feet are, we are happy and enjoying life's adventures together. I truly hope that, if in the end nothing else, our friendship can endure and that this man will always be a part of my life, and AJ's. A "lifer," as I call them.

And there you have it. This is my spreadsheet of men. Not so slutty after all, right? Not even by a long shot if you consider some of the shocking stories you sometimes hear of what goes on in the online dating world. Mine has been pretty meek, and I'm grateful for that. I must add that recently, a friend sent me a meme that said something like, "Ladies!! Stop screwing around with the leftovers on online dating sites. Start prowling the obituaries! Look for 'She leaves behind a wonderful, loving and supportive husband.'" Kinda tacky, maybe, but I'm thinking perhaps we give it a go. I can't handle much more of this simply fun and games at this point in my life. I don't want any drama or complications I have to navigate. I have had enough of that already. I just want to be at peace. This girl wants to be loved completely and correctly or left the fuck alone.

No more sex, drugs, and rock n roll. I want sex, cuddles, support, and peace.

Chapter 13

I'm Not Intimidating. You're IntimidaTED!

We live in a world filled with double standards.

Man sleeps around - stud. Woman sleeps around - whore.

Man raises his voice - demands respect. Woman raises her voice - overbearing bitch.

Man cries - crybaby/momma's boy. Woman cries - typical normal, sensitive emotional shit.

Man staying at home looking after children - probably couldn't make it as a man out in the business world or poor thing! Look at him having to maintain the home because his wife chose her career. Woman staying at home looking after children - expected but also, must be nice.

Man rises to the executive level in a company - respect. Woman rises to the executive level in a company - wonder who she slept with to get the job, and God forbid you have kids because then it's the added "*those poor kids will have to raise themselves*" or her poor husband having to carry the household load.

Man forces himself onto a woman - rapist. Woman forces herself onto a man - who cares, or what man wouldn't want it, right? Women may be labeled as "overly emotional" or "too direct," while men exhibiting similar behaviors are often seen as "passionate" or "decisive."

One of my medical directors witnessed me really getting beat up on a call one day and told I was being awfully aggressive. After the call he sent me a private message asking, "*What is the difference between being seen as assertive and being seen as aggressive? Gender!*" Man, was he spot on! A woman who sets clear expectations, communicates directly, and holds people accountable is an aggressive bitch. While a man doing the exact same things is simply an astute businessman.

So very many double standards both ways. However, I can't help but feel like we, as women, bear the brunt of it partially because we get it from everywhere! The men who don't want us there. The women who got there and don't want any competition to stay there. Hell, our own parents who see our way of life as choosing a career over family because we work and have big jobs. It's like they're proud on one level, but then comes the "*Just don't forget you only have a 5-year-old once*". Or "*There are only so many school plays and sporting events you get to attend.*" In the end, the reactions of both men and women are brought on by decades and decades of indoctrination from one generation to the next about what your role should be in society, within the family, and within a marriage. Times are changing, though. Thank God for that! We're certainly not there yet, but at least there has been some movement in the right direction.

Even so, women are still expected to behave a certain way, dress a certain way, and talk a certain way. If you color outside the lines, you get called bossy, bitchy, aggressive, too sensitive, etc.

Adding to this, the fact that people tend to project their own insecurities on others by calling them names or trying to degrade them to deflect from their own perceived shortcomings just makes life in the corporate world that much more challenging. It's not just in the corporate world, but outside of the office too. At least outside of the office, I can tell Karen to fuck off without having to face an arduous meeting with HR.

People feel intimidated by me just because of my title. For the longest time, I wondered what it was that I was putting out there to make others think that I was intimidating. I've had people tell me things like, "Oh, I thought you were such a snob when I first met you." Um, thank you? I mean, really. Were you raised in a barn? Are you going to mistakenly ask if I'm pregnant next?

When I saw Oprah interview Michelle Obama, she asked how she got over feeling intimidated sitting at big tables filled with smart, powerful men. Michelle said, "You realize pretty quickly that a lot of them aren't that smart." I think about that quote quite often. I've realized a lot of folks in important roles with big titles are actually very small people, not in size (although, as established earlier, I do firmly believe this would be the case if the size of men's appendages were as prominently displayed as some of ours), but in knowledge, experience, background, and maturity. Those tables where you feel you don't belong, actually need you desperately. They need you because they need someone who knows how to run the business. Someone who truly understands the operations or the functionality and has the knowledge to keep the train on the tracks. What's really scary is when they don't know they need you. When decisions are made in silos without anyone at the table who really understands the inner workings of the business, look out because it will all eventually come crashing down. After all, even the Roman Empire eventually fell.

It took me a long time to learn that how others perceive me actually has very little to do with me. Their perception is a culmination of their own personality, historical experiences, traumas, insecurities, level of maturity, and baggage combined. You can aim to be the sweetest, most caring, and helpful person in the world and still be perceived as a threat by someone who sees the world as threatening. The thing is, others' opinions hold little value. We get so caught up in what others think of us that we lose ourselves in trying to fit a specific mold. People donate to political campaigns, attend events for people they do not agree with, and donate massive amounts of money just to win their favor! People sit at the table with individuals they cannot stand and do not respect just to be seen as part of the "in crowd." I've never cared to be popular and never been willing or honestly able to "fake it til I make it." For exactly that reason, 95% of the people in my life are acquaintances, not friends. Sadly, some of them were dear friends or even family at one point. Still, because of my inability or unwillingness to add more superficial relationships, they went from the inner circle to the outer. These instances have sometimes broken my heart, but in the end, being my authentic self is more important to me than some photo opportunity for Instagram, or my loss of self-respect for allowing less than I need or deserve to be the norm!

I AM a lot! They're right. I have a lot of layers. A lot of personality. A lot of dreams. A lot of ideas. A lot of feelings. A lot of love. I have a lot to give! So, when someone says that I'm too much, I've learned those are not my people. I've learned to smile and invite them to go find less because I'm not going to make myself less of a person for them. Not anymore. I'm sad that you see me as competition. That my light shines too bright for you. There is enough sunshine for all of us to shine together, but I will not dim my light or reduce myself to a shadow for your comfort.

When someone tells you that you're intimidating, tell them, "No, you're intimidaTED!" There's a difference.

Stop taking on others' insecurities, immaturities, and perceived shortcomings when they try to have you carry it for them by way of calling you names.

To the women who are labeled aggressive – keep being assertive.

To the women who are labeled bossy – keep on leading.

To the women who are labeled difficult – keep telling the truth.

To the women who are labeled too much – keep taking up space.

To the women who are labeled complicated – keep asking hard questions.

Remember, use your voice! Even if it shakes!

Sometimes, I find myself asking why life can be so challenging. We're all familiar with the quote, "*To Whom Much is Given, Much Is Required.*" Jesus said this about two thousand years ago. Sidebar…I'd been working a year at the county hospital where I live, and most patients speak Spanish. I didn't speak a word when I got there and had to learn trial by fire because most of the staff there also preferred Spanish. As a result, I cannot converse with you in Spanish, but I can explain just about any medical condition or procedure pretty damn well. If you sing Figaro as Sylvester does to Tweety, BOOM Higado (liver in Spanish), you will never mispronounce that shit again! I knew it was time to go when I misread a t-shirt. Do you remember when "Vote for Pedro" was super popular because of the movie Napoleon Dynamite? Yeah, well, I'm walking down the hallway with the cath-lab team and pass a kid wearing a shirt that says in bright red letters, "Vote for Jesus." No joke, the token white girl of the group says, yes, out loud for all to hear: who's Jesus?

(pronounced "Hey-Soos") Blond, not stupid...I swear!! Anyhoo, President John F. Kennedy also quoted this verse in a speech in 1963 at Vanderbilt. Although this is a guiding principle of mine, I tend to better identify and lean on the idea that "*You cannot wish for both strong character and an easy life. The price of each is the other.*" Back to the whole being able to look myself in the mirror thing.

I refuse to make myself smaller just to make someone else feel better about themselves. If others make you feel small, then maybe you should invest more time and effort in your own growth. We too easily get caught up in everything and everyone *outside* of us. You will spend far more time in this life speaking to yourself in your own head than you will with anyone else. Stop telling yourself that you're "too" something. Too loud, too out there, too ambitious, too caring, too straight, too gay, too ugly, too fat, too liberal, too conservative, too open, too whatever. You're not too anything. You're YOU! No one can be more youer than you, as Dr. Seuss would say. This is your superpower. No one else has the experience, the knowledge, the thoughts, the ideas, the personality, and the vision you have. There may be certain similarities. But you, as a package, are one of a kind!

To me, the ultimate success looks like achieving my greatest potential while being entirely true to myself. I want to be wildly successful while being as me as I can possibly be.

Do *NOT* spend your precious and finite time on Earth as a watered-down version of yourself to attempt to "fit in" or make others comfortable. That is the opposite of being true to you. Fitting in is the opposite of being your authentic self! Do not fall into that trap. They can accept all of you or miss out on all of you! It really is that simple. Some people are going to reject you because you shine too bright for them. That's okay. They don't pay your electric bill. Shine on!

Public service announcement: I don't care if you think how I carry myself makes me look like I think I'm better than you. Take that shit to a therapist and get better soon. It's 2024. We ain't making ourselves small to accommodate your insecurities.

We, as humans, tend to make life far more complicated than it really is. I believe that everyone should be forced to go to therapy at least once a year. That way, we can all learn how to heal ourselves and stop expecting others to do it for us. It takes a tremendous amount of courage to be able to look in the mirror and recognize the part you play in keeping yourself a slave to your own insecurities. None of us are perfect, but every single human being on this planet can learn.

Don't know how to overcome your insecurities? Learn! Don't know how to say no? Learn! Don't know how to be accepting of yourself? Learn!

The internet is right at your fingertips, filled with resources out the wazoo. I can almost guarantee that there is not a single topic that is not covered on some website. You can learn how to overcome anxiety to feel more secure and confident in your interactions with others. You can learn how to regulate your own emotions so others don't trigger you and cause you to break down or act out. You can learn how to overcome traumas you've experienced in your childhood so you don't become a people pleaser who gets treated like a doormat by a long line of undeserving people.

You can learn how to be secure within yourself. She's not born with it, and it's not Maybelline. It's inner work is what it is. And remember, it's hard, but the work works!

I joke that I am a CEO because "badass miracle worker" isn't an official job title! And I know I'm cute because if I weren't, why would all these websites be offering me cookies all the time? Accept the cookies and go learn!!

Women often downplay their skills or achievements in professional settings so they don't come across as being too ambitious, which some might find intimidating. This type of self-diminishing behavior often includes softening their voice, not speaking up in meetings, and giving others credit for their work. All because of someone else's needs, wants, and opinions. It's bullshit. It's prevalent, but it's prevalent bullshit. If you have a picture forming in your head of a world filled with super assertive, outgoing, boss bitch babes, that's not what I'm trying to say at all. I'm trying to bring across that we should learn how to be comfortable with who we are as individuals while striving to continually grow and better ourselves, while giving others the grace to do the same.

We need to do better as a society. We need to become more aware, practice more critical thinking skills, learn how to deal with our emotions and support one another without fearing they may take something away from us. Yes, in a way, it's a dog-eat-dog world out there. But at the same time, we're kind of all in this together. No one gets out of this experience alive, and it could end at any moment. Do you want to live your life cowering from your highest self? Your purpose, your potential, your life? There's a major difference between living and existing. I don't want to merely exist. I don't want to run like a lab rat on a spinning wheel, to and fro between work and home like some zombie. I want to take up space and live my life as my authentic self to the fullest. I want to learn, make mistakes, stand up, and have my voice heard. I want to be seen, loved, and acknowledged. I want to inspire both myself and others. I don't want to hide due to fear. So often what we fear could happen, never comes to fruition anyway. We spend so much of our precious time not doing the things we want to do because we are afraid of what people will think or what might go wrong. What if what happens is amazing? What if we do the thing that scares the ever-living shit out of us and it goes great? To miss out on something amazing because we are afraid of a less than desirable outcome, that for all intents and purposes will never even happen, is exactly how we end up surviving life instead of living it!

Ever heard that saying fear is a liar? He is!! An absolute flat out pathological liar! I shared a favorite line of mine earlier in the book where Kevin Hart said, "my belly button fell through my asshole". Go look up the video. I'm sure there will be plenty of opinions here when I tell you that AJ is the one that showed me this video. We were on one of our momma AJ trips and were waiting in line for one of the big rides at an amusement park. He pulls up this video of a stand-up routine of Kevin Hart's. He is talking about when he was in Japan for a business trip and went to a big amusement park over there. He describes how in the United States they pull the bar down over your head and you feel safe when you hear the click click. Kevin had been seated on one of the coasters and pulled the bar down over his head and…NO click click! He said he kept pulling it up and down and nothing. You can hear in his voice the fear that was building in him as he couldn't get it to secure. He shared how he thought in that moment, well, this is it. I die on a ride in one of the most technologically advanced countries in the world because of no click click! He demonstrates on stage how he's nearly hysterical trying to flag down one of the workers and that eventually a young man working the ride comes over and gives him a thumbs up and in a very heavy Japanese accent says, "so excited!" With that, the tram pulls out and he realizes that he's not on the ride and about to die. He's simply on the tram TO the ride. I LOVED this video for two reasons. One because it made me laugh so hard, I thought I'd pee in my pants and two because it honestly taught me something. Fear and excitement feel the same to our minds and our bodies. Sweaty palms, pounding heart, flushed face, hummidititties, and bellybutton in the asshole! I've been making a concerted effort ever since to say, "I'm so excited" instead of "I'm so afraid" "I'm thrilled" instead of "I'm terrified". And by the way, AJ and I say "so excited" in that hilarious accent to each other about scary things to this day. Come to think of it, I'm sure people wonder what in the world is wrong with us because these are often our words to each other in scary situations. Me going in for a biopsy and AJ and I saying "so excited" as our final words. AJ walking into school on the day of standardized testing…"so excited".

It's scary. I never said it wasn't. Standing up in a meeting to have your voice heard can be extremely intimidating. Saying no for the first time can make you feel like you're about to have a heart attack. Picking your own mental/emotional/physical well-being above others is foreign to so many of us, myself included. But I've learned that if my cup is empty, how the hell do I help fill yours? If I'm sick and tired, how do I care for you when you are? If I'm dead, who's going to help you then? Allowing yourself to lower your defense mechanisms so others may see you as you truly are can be overwhelming. But do you really want to live a life being less than what you're capable of merely because of forces outside of yourself?

There will always be those who criticize, those who point and laugh, those who drag others down, those who project their own insecurities, those who do not want to see you succeed, and those who try to make you feel less worthy. Let them. I listened to an episode of Mel Robbins' podcast (I'm a freak-level fan and aspire to be on her podcast one day), and she was sharing an idea about the concept of "Let Them." I debated having a "let them" tattoo on one inner arm and "I am enough" on the other, but I'm still tattoo-free. The idea is whatever other people want to do or say to you…let them. Let them forget to include you. Let them flat-out exclude you. Let them keep their head in the sand and refuse to see the dysfunction. Let them miss out on you! Just LET THEM!!!

Learn how not to allow it to make you make yourself smaller. Quit trying to change the minds of folks. You aren't the jackass whisperer!

I'm not intimidating. You're intimidaTED!

Shine sister! Shine for the whole world to see your light!

"Whack-a-mole"

This was one of those "AHA moments," as Oprah calls them. AJ and I were on a mama/AJ date, as we call them, at a pizza spot he loves that has a whole arcade full of games and little prizes you get from winning tickets at the games. You know what I'm talking about. It's the place where you spend $100 on game tokens so your kid wins enough to get the prized item they're eyeing that you could've paid $4 for at the discount chain store. Yeah. That place. I stood watching as he played this game called "whack-a-mole." I'm sure you know it. Literally beating the ever-living shit out of these poor plastic versions of burrowing mammals as their beady little eyes plead for grace. One pops up, WHACK. Another one shows his head, WHACK. I stood there and thought, Man, alive, I'm a fucking mole! Good thing I didn't say it out loud right then. *I'm a mole!* Not in the cool, hot spy lady sense, either. More in the raggedy, beaten down, blue-eyed lady looking at life and asking for a little grace.

I'd said for a couple of years I'd gone pretty quiet at work because high performance and industry knowledge leading to suggestions for change wasn't what they wanted. Disrupters looking to continue to improve and develop weren't what was desired. It was quiet, yes people to smile and kid and stroke the egos of those weaponized incompetents we discussed in an earlier chapter. It takes a toll on morale when "leaders" play whack-a-mole with their people. Keep the reality quiet so everything looks good while those on the front line drown and die a slow, painful death.

Transfer whack-a-mole to family or friendships when you come with your hat in hand to discuss important topics or shed light on something, and it's that much more painful. What's sad is when the moles stop coming up for air. When they decide, burrowing and staying hidden for their mental health and safety is what's in their best interest. We stop speaking up. We stop adding to the friend and family group threads—no more sharing accomplishments or troubled moments when we need support. We just go quiet. We handle everything ourselves. When the moles burrow and stop coming up for air, companies lose the really great people one after another; Friendships change or end; Families break apart.

There will always be those who will try to drag you down. The people on their high horses need to be reminded that it's a long way down when they fall off that horse. And they WILL eventually fall. Tuck and roll, Karen!

Some people are just lollipops of fun triple-dipped in psycho sauce, and there is literally nothing you can do to change that. So when they push your buttons or set a negative narrative about you....just let them. The less you care, the less impact it has on you, your life, and your performance.

Sometimes the appropriate serenity prayer for us when we have to deal with these folks is, "*Lord, grant me the serenity to accept (assholes, incompetents, narcissists, stupid Mofos) as they are* (let them), *the courage and restraint to maintain my self-control, and wisdom to know that if I act on it, I'll go to jail.*" Amen. I've already made y'all aware that orange is not my color.

We've established that setbacks in life can be good and serve their own purpose. These setbacks often show us our strengths. When life knocks you down, stand the fuck back up and say, "*You hit like a bitch.*" Not a boss bitch, just a little bitch. Two very different things. Take those hits or unfounded ugly criticisms and turn them into paper airplanes. Now you can consider them flying fucks.

Chapter 14

Allie's 3 Rules

We all need rules to live by. I have two separate sets of rules. Three rules in life and three rules in business. These rules can be applied to different situations in different areas of life to ensure we leave it in a better condition than we found it.

In Business - Pretty much anyone on my A-Team could likely recite these by memory. I share these at every new facility kick off and new hire orientation I participate in, and they haven't changed in years. I tell people that if they can understand and own my three rules, they will be very successful in their roles and we will be even more successful together!

Rule #1: Don't lie.

This includes not trying to hide mistakes. One mistake or one moment where you screw up doesn't define you. I screw up somewhere in my life on some level every day. But I own it. I apologize where appropriate, try to learn from it, and pick something else to screw up tomorrow. Make your mess your message. Accountability is key. Don't try to hide the error you made or try to sweep it under the rug. Don't tell me you can't make it to work because your uncle died when he already died four times earlier in the year. Don't say you know how to do something you don't know how to do.

Rule #2: Don't steal.

Don't steal stuff. It's pretty obvious not to walk out with the training laptop or a box of masks at the peak of COVID-19. Also, it should be obvious, but don't steal other people's ideas and present them as your own. Don't steal credit. Don't steal resources by being late all the time or hogging the one tech in the emergency department that day. Or monopolizing the time of the one admin assistant set to support the entire team. Don't steal other people's joy. When people work hard, THANK THEM, and mean it!

Rule #3: Every job under this roof belongs to everyone under this roof unless it is legally outside your scope of practice.

Have you ever seen those memes where it's someone's job to paint those lines on the road, and they paint over roadkill, with the tagline: "It's not my job." That's what I'm talking about. Unless the task falls outside the legal scope of your expertise, there's no such thing as "it's not my job." We're all in this together and will work together to support one another as any true team does. Do you want to earn true respect and loyalty from your team to last a lifetime? Don't be afraid to get your hands dirty. Let them see you pushing the mop bucket in your high heels because there's a clean-up on aisle three (vomit in the waiting room), and everyone but you is busy. Respond to that call from a team member in a patient room in your dress and throw those gloves on to assist in moving a patient. Let your medics on shift come out and help you unload the ventilator and oxygen tank from the back of your vehicle during Covid because they needed one, and another facility had an extra one available. (Please don't call CMS or TXDOT; it was a crisis!) My examples of this come from my time in hospital administration, but you get my drift! If you want team players, then BE one! It's not that complicated, right, and yet so many "leaders" don't get it. People can quote books until they're purple in the face, but reading a book and doing a presentation on servant leadership doesn't make you one. And worse yet, when you're up there preaching as the leader of the organization but the team you've put together to your left and right don't exhibit those same attributes, you might as well forgo the presentation because I assure you everyone in the room knows it!

In Life

Rule #1: Just be kind.

Be kind, just because you can. Give a shit. If you don't have anything nice to say, just shut the fuck up. Realize that words matter. A lot! A genuine compliment or words of encouragement can make a massive difference in someone else's life, even if you don't realize it. It costs a grand total of $0 just to be kind. Praise in public and chastise in private. Don't think that saying "not to call you out or put you on the spot" just before doing precisely that changes anything. Trust me when I tell you that being kind is FREE. And the opposite is true for the assholes. It will cost you dearly. Monetarily, when you have a revolving door of people who have to be replaced or people that you have whack-a-mole'd into silence who quit striving to perform at a high level and silently leave. It will cost you when that bestie, partner, or family member finally walks away because they simply cannot take it anymore. Being an asshole is more costly than you might realize!

Just being kind can go a long way and make a big difference in someone else's life. It doesn't even take much effort. For example, I unexpectedly received a card from a good friend of mine's husband when my divorce started. On the card, it said: "*Despite it all, remember a couple of things. You are a tremendous mother, you are a hot little biscuit, and you are the baddest bitch in the building! No one can take those things away from you.*"

Another favorite of mine comes from my favorite barista at my neighborhood Starbucks. I hadn't been in several months. Crazy, I know. But I pulled up and ordered, which wasn't even my standard daily order. But the sweet little voice on the drive-thru speaker exclaimed, "Allie, is that you?" I said oh my gosh, yes! When I got up to the window, sweet Claire practically came through the window to squeeze my arm and say she'd been missing me. She gave me my birthday latte and made me feel so special! What a way to start the day.

Rule #2: Don't hurt people.

We should all take the Hippocratic oath that says, "*First, do no harm.*" I don't wake up plotting who I will hurt today and how. Only an assholic psychopath does that. We have all off days, so take a step back and a moment to breathe. If you're super angry or frustrated, institute my 24hr rule where I hold off and contemplate the topic. After 24hrs if i'm still convinced it is a major time, then respond as such. But don't react in the moment and risk saying or doing things you cannot take back. Don't launch a text thread attacking someone to their core because you're having a bad day/week/month/life. Don't make it worse. Don't hurt. Don't harm. It's pretty simple.

Rule #3: Try to help where you can

It's good to be kind. If you can't help me, at least don't harm me. If you can't fix my challenge, just point me in the direction of someone who can. However, if you do have the ability to assist, do so whenever you can. Whether through simple encouragement, financial or economic assistance, or even just lending an ear, we are all uniquely positioned to help others at different points in our lives. Now that being said... boundaries are a must!

Boundaries, People! Boundaries!

In addition to the rules described above, I've more recently learned about the importance of establishing and, more importantly, enforcing boundaries. Boundaries for work. Boundaries for friends. Boundaries for family. Hell, boundaries for yourself!

If you're anything like me, when I was first exposed to the concept, I was like, "What are these 'boundaries' you speak of?" Essentially, think of them as your rules of engagement with yourself and others. What you are willing to accept and what you aren't. What you are willing to give and what you are not. I sure wish someone had taken the time to share this concept with me before my mid-40s! Imagine all the extra money I'd have? The extra time! The extra sanity, for god's sake!

You may wonder about the boundaries for yourself, especially because why on Earth would we need boundaries for ourselves? Well, for me, it's because I'm a fixer. Give me a problem or a set of circumstances, and I will develop a way out. Plan a course of action to "fix it." I went on two dates with you, and you got a DUI and are at risk of losing your nursing license because it's not your first; sure, call me, and I'll figure it out. You're one who consistently and thematically makes poor choices and then needs your person to be there to carry you through it and listen to your Groundhog Day saga. Sure, I got you. You're a boss that is in way over their head and out of their league but will simply not ask for help. Sure, just steal my work and make it your own. You're a raging narcissist who gaslights and triangulates. I'm here for ya! It's like one of my favorite scenes from Steel Magnolias where M'Lynn says, *"I just wanna hit somebody until they feel as bad as I do. I just wanna hit something! I wanna hit it hard!"* And Cheree grabs Ouiser, holding her in front of M'Lynn, yelling, *"Here! Hit this! Go ahead, M'Lynn, slap her! We'll sell T-shirts saying, 'I slapped Ouiser Boudreaux!' HIT HER! Knock her out! Here! Hit Ouiser!"*

How does this apply, you ask?? I'm sick and fucking tired of being Ouiser!

About the same time as my mid-life "revolution" (because it wasn't a crisis, but rather an awakening), I realized I was going to continue getting used and abused and getting the proverbial shit kicked out of me regularly unless I took control of my life and set some major boundaries with those who are in it. Some of these resulted in great changes, and others not so great. Some were incredibly painful and heartbreaking. For instance, you're not as popular at work when you're not a yes person, but rather one that questions and pushes the bar on the status quo. Your relationships change when you're no longer the rescuer for the habitually needy. It can be highly disruptive when you've been in an incredibly dysfunctional boat with family or friends and choose to finally step out of that boat. The folks who choose to stay in the boat can't figure out what the hell is wrong with you and why you've removed yourself. Some are hurt by your departure, while others become angry and go so far as to sabotage your choice. And man, oh man, once you've disembarked from the crazy train and seen the light, there's no unseeing it. You can't just go back and pretend the epiphany never happened and all is well with the world again. Nor can you force those remaining steadfast passengers to see what they don't want or aren't capable of seeing. THAT is painful. Through lots of research and reading I learned two things that I've clung to in an effort to help me maintain the progress I've made rather than reverting back and to continue my healing journey. Both of these examples seem obvious, but helped me tremendously. One I learned while listening to the coaching sessions in Mel Robbin's book Kick Ass. The realization that simultaneously loving someone very much, but also being mad as hell at that person doesn't make me crazy. It makes me normal. And the other from listening to Dr. Sherrie Campbell where she discusses loving someone from a distance. That we can love someone, and still for our own mental and emotional well being, NOT reconcile. When the other individual in a relationship sees nothing wrong with their behavior and demonstrates no true remorse for their actions or desire to change going forward, our emotional/mental/ physical safety must come first. On a positive note, I've made massive progress in understanding my value. I can do more than ever for those I truly love and care for because I'm so much more selective of who those folks are.

Boundaries for work? Unless you are self-employed, we all have bosses, managers, or boards to whom we report and to whom we must answer. However, this doesn't mean you can't or shouldn't have boundaries there. Every decision I make professionally is made with the idea that I always want to look at myself in the mirror and be proud of who I am and the choices I've made. I have a strong spidey sense, and I'm almost always spot on when things don't feel right. If it looks/smells like a big pile of shit, it probably is just that. I've left several positions during my tenure on the operations side of things because of just that. Don't get bamboozled into going along with something because it's above your pay grade. Unless, of course, orange IS your color, and you're good with ignoring your moral compass. Don't allow folks to be treated as less than they deserve just because that's how some of those above you behave. In the end, we ALL have voices, but only the bravest tend to use them when risks or consequences are associated with doing so.

My most recent experience with this was during the fourth and final interview for a larger role in a large healthcare company. I was asked for some feedback on why I thought certain things were happening or about the overall direction of the organization. In that instant, I knew if I was honest and used my voice, this opportunity would be gone. I also knew I wouldn't respect myself if I decided to remain silent to secure the position, so I spoke the truth. One of my favorite RBG quotes is, "Don't be afraid to use your voice even if it shakes." Mine was slow and steady, and I shared a great deal. I was thanked very much for my candid feedback and told he'd be in touch within a week after looking into the feedback I'd provided. Luckily, I knew enough to know I'd never hear back from him on what I'd spoken up on and didn't hold my breath. We've established orange is not my color, but neither is blue! Sadly, I never did hear back from him, but I take solace that 1) I was 100% honest AND was true to myself and 2) I know deep down inside he knows it too. I didn't get the role, and nothing changed. Great people kept leaving. Silos kept building. Sadly, I just think that even Rome fell, so eventually, so will that place. In fact, the man hired for that very position faced much of what I'd shared so openly with the CEO during my interview and was only with the organization for about a year. Five bosses in as many years screams problem, but not when no one is listening.

However, I kept my word to myself to always do my best and do what's right in every circumstance I'm presented with! Work boundaries also include for me the need to realize that I couldn't be "on" 24/7/365! I mean, hell, my tagline with my team is that my door is always open, and my phone is always on! While I take that quite literally and very seriously, I realized I might have gone just a bit too far in that pledge. Picture this: El Paso, Texas, 2023, and I'm being a good, health-conscious woman getting my annual mammogram. I'm literally in the middle of the exam. Yes, butt naked other than a waist gown with a boob pancaked and all, and I got a call that came through on my Apple watch. What did I do? I answered the call from the director of case management. I will admit the laughs that ensued by both her and the mammo tech made it worth the ridiculousness of my actions. But I realized how completely out of control this had gotten. Really, Allie? A call from corporate can't wait for the steamrolling of my right boob to conclude? What in the actual fuck?

Last but certainly not least, the boundaries you set for others. It's important to understand that although we're setting boundaries for other people, these are just our rules of engagement for what we will and will not accept from them. We all have rough times in our lives, and it's wonderful to be in a place where you can assist, but there must be limits. Especially for us givers and fixers because the takers have no limits. For that employee who borrowed $1k when they were in a rough patch, I'm willing to forgive the debt that they never mentioned or repaid, but I'll never be willing to loan them money again. People who constantly run late for meetings. You can say something like, "*I would love to catch up, but now I only have about twenty minutes since you were a bit behind.*" That person who rants at you and says hurtful, ugly things leaves you in a puddle of tears while they're completely fine after having said their piece. You can remove yourself from their life completely. You can avoid situations where those tantrums seem to be triggered. You can have a conversation saying, "*I care for you/I love you/I respect you* (depending on the relationship in peril), *but I simply cannot continue to be on the receiving end of your attacks.*" This puts the ball in their court to own their behavior, apologize, and make the necessary adjustments to keep you in their life. Otherwise, toodaloo mothafucka!

Sadly, in all seriousness, if they are incapable of such, it may be painful, but you will know that you gave them every opportunity to continue to be in your life. Some people truly are incapable of even acknowledging their wrong doing, let alone owning it and offering an apology. A genuine apology includes three parts in my mind. It starts with I'm sorry….then in the middle sits what they are apologizing for…and lastly is a changed behavior so that it does not recur. For example, "I'm so sorry for being late, but I'm going to add extra time to get here in the future". Someone who states "Geez, I'm sorry. You get so upset over nothing dude. Calm down." is not sorry, will never be sorry, and will likely always be late. This is perhaps an overly simplified example, but the idea holds true regardless of the infraction. Someone saying I'm sorry for whatever you think I did?? The person who does or says something terrible and says I have no idea what you want me to be sorry for?? The infamous I'm sorry but…followed by what you did to seemingly deserve it?? These are not apologies and are not coming from someone likely to be capable of feeling remorse or of making the needed change. Some people just have to be loved from a distance. It's like touching a hot stove. How many times do you burn yourself before you step back and put on a glove (explaining your boundary) or stop touching the stove at all (walking away when they aren't willing or able to change)?

What are your rules in life? Have you ever given it any thought? If you had to write out a list of rules you want yourself and the people in your life to live by, what would they be? Give it some thought. These should be based on your personal values. Do you know what your values are in life? Few people are taught to figure out their values and live by them. It's important, though. It's your compass; without it, you're just plodding along in a random direction in life. Spinning in circles on that hamster wheel with no direction or clear path in sight.

It all comes down to what is most important to you. Is it your health? Wealth? Family? Career? Faith? Your fucking sanity?

Knowing what you value in life will help you plot a course that heads in a direction that will be most fulfilling to you. If you're working yourself to the bone in a job you don't like or value, why keep doing it when there are so many other choices and opportunities out in the world?

What about your health? Do you value your health? Then put down that cheeseburger, missy. Live in alignment with your values. FYI…perhaps I value my thick thighs!!

When setting boundaries, I have learned that you can follow a few simple steps to make it a little easier to communicate. If you're not familiar with using "I feel" language, it's a common tool used in psychology to communicate your needs in a manner that makes someone more open to receiving it. It makes your request come across as less "demanding." There are three parts to it. Here's how it works.

I feel….(frustrated)

When you….(talk over me)

Because….(it's disrespectful)

Next time, please….(allow me to finish talking)

So you start off by saying how you feel, for example, "*I feel dismissed.*" Now, just saying how you feel without indicating what the other person did to make you feel this way might make them feel a bit confused. This might sound like: "*When you don't include me in the decision-making process.*" Then, lastly, you want to explain why this action makes you feel this way. For example, "*Because it makes me feel like you don't value my input.*"

The boundary then comes in by stating what you want them to do next time instead of what they did the previous time. For example: "*Next time, please include me in the decision-making process.*" Try to focus on what you want them to do instead of what you don't want them to do. How do you feel when I phrase the same request in the negative: "*Next time, don't do that.*" Did it feel different? Did it make you feel a little obsessively defiant or like you want to double down?

Next, and this is the most important part, is to enforce this boundary when your person doesn't do what they agreed to. So, when they cross this boundary again (which could be purely because they'd forgotten or because they're used to doing something a certain way and not because they are being spiteful), remind them of the boundary you agreed on. I generally give someone two strikes, and then they're out. Maybe you're more lenient, but the main point is that if they consistently ignore your boundaries, you need to walk away because it means this person is choosing not to be respectful of your preferences.

And remember, someone can disagree with your boundaries but still respect them.

Now, go be a badass boundary boss out there!

Chapter 15

Mom's Suitcase

Have you read anything about empaths before? If so, then you likely read an absolute description of my mom. *Maybe* even saw her picture next to the description of the word. Empaths can feel what others are feeling so deeply that they "absorb" or "take on" the emotions themselves, often to the degree that can be detrimental to their own mental and emotional well-being. I've never known someone to take on other people's feelings like my mom. She takes them on not just to the point she shares in the feelings; she owns them and then somehow feels accountable for them as well. With the dynamics in my family, at times, this has caused and cost her a lot. Sometimes heartache. Sometimes, some sanity. Sometimes, it impacts her own health, physical, emotional, and even mental.

She has always claimed that the most impactful thing she's learned from me is that you cannot tell someone else how to feel. It is always funny to me when she says that because she feels so deeply, but I do remember the moment that produced that statement from me. I was probably 14 or 15 years old and felt extremely hurt over a situation with the two musketeers in the house: my dad and my brother. I asked something along the lines of why my dad loved my brother so much more than me. Why everything was always my fault when it came to him? Or how situations that occurred and my feelings about them were always excused with statements such as "*You know how he is*" or, "*That's just* him", or "Don't take it so personally." She said that I shouldn't feel that way. I remember standing in the hallway outside my bedroom door while ugly crying with snot running down my upper lip, yelling, "*Don't you tell me how to feel. My feelings are mine whether anyone else can see it or not.*" Pretty profound for a teenager and I think I forgot that somewhere along the way while striving to do better, to do more, to do whatever it took to be seen and loved by my father.

As a mama myself, I realize her comments were meant to comfort me in my hurt. However, as an adult who has read a lot about healing and self-work, I know now that when we say, "That's not true" or "Don't feel that way," when someone shares something with us, we invalidate their feelings. This family dynamic has continued throughout my lifetime, and my mom's attempt to push for respect, kindness, and acceptance for me has had truly profound consequences on her. She adores "her boyfriend," as she's always referred to my dad, despite close to 50 years of marriage, and she loves both of her children, myself and my brother, desperately. However, the love she has for my son, my why and often hers, is like nothing I've ever seen. AJ has some characteristics similar to those of she and my brother that have historically made our family challenging to understand and navigate. Her empathy has become so intense on the topic that she blames herself entirely.

I say to her regularly that we all have different genetic predispositions, etc. Although they may play a part in our overall makeup, we are all responsible for our behavior and choices. To see this woman suffer the way she has with the weight of so much unfounded and unjust guilt has been heartbreaking. The toll it has taken on her and the manifestations of that are immense. My mom had kept an impeccably clean house. Played the hostess with the mostest for after-symphony parties that were legendary. No catering and service folks hired over here! Just mom running around like a chicken without a head, making sure everything was perfect! Decor, food, music, conversation, and most spectacularly, this uncanny air about her that always made everyone feel welcome and loved. Mom taught primary school-age kids for more than 35 years and would regularly receive college graduation or wedding invitations from former students. Imagine a teacher so impacting you in the second grade that 15 to 20 years later, you wanted them to attend such a monumental event in your life. That's my mom. I used to laugh, and if I'm honest, roll my eyes a bit because literally everywhere we went, someone would stop her and hug her and say, *"You were the best teacher I ever had."*

One of her biggest talents and specialties was working with kids with dyslexia or other major challenges with reading. For whatever reason, AJ has never been willing or allowed my mom to coach him on this. It breaks my mom's heart because she feels certain she could really assist, so she has a deep sadness and feeling of helplessness regarding the topic. I've tried a handful of times to discuss it with AJ, but he just won't have it. I try to encourage my mom to just simply be AJ's MeMe (as they spell it) and enjoy her time with this amazing boy. Sadly, she just can't seem to do that. She pushes and pulls and tries to get him to work with her on it, and it usually ends in an argument or a complete blow-up, by both of them. She often talks about how AJ can't read and if he'd just let her help him, she could. I've told her repeatedly that he reads just fine, when there is something he WANTS to read. I was thrilled as was AJ when he passed the reading and math portions of the standardized tests, he took this last year with a "mastery" rating for his age group! Don't worry MeMe, AJ is doing just fine!

A pretty extreme example of people from everywhere knowing and loving my mom took place on one of the scariest nights of my life. AJ was maybe three years old and had an unbreakable fever. His dad and I were just terrified as they transferred us via ambulance from the ER in the hospital where he worked to the PICU at their sister facility. I remember driving across town behind that ambulance with my son and then-husband inside, praying to God that if this was it, to please take me instead and if he really had to have his son back now, to please take me with him. He'd had a fever of 105.9 for hours on end that wouldn't break. I'd text my hospital colleagues and physician friends and was able to get one of the best doctors in town to meet us at the receiving hospital. I'll never forget when he walked into our room and saw my mom, AJ's "*MiMi*." He went straight to her and just about picked her up with a hug. She immediately said oh my gosh! How is Sam?! She had apparently, but not at all surprisingly, had an enormous impact on his youngest son, Sam. Life-changing in his words. He turned his focus to AJ but told me he knew of me and respected me because of my reputation in the community, but that now that he knew I was Mrs. Trimble's daughter, he would be forever in my debt. We spent a week in the hospital, and AJ came out of it all just fine, other than having an incredible fear of hospitals! But that's my mom. More than twenty years after the fact, a parent pledged everything he had because of how she had impacted his child!

It literally makes me feel sick at times when I see how this once powerhouse version of my mom has devolved over the years into a fragile, emotional shell of her former self. There are times I see her and my heart just breaks because she doesn't even look like my mom. Worse yet is how those who really helped push her to this stage look at her and see an emotionally damaged, often depressed, mild hypochondriac who has become a recluse in her own home. A once very social person who now prefers not to leave the house other than when absolutely necessary. She was often home alone with my brother and me because Dad had symphony practice in the evenings and played golf on the weekends. She will tell you she never had the luxury of making or maintaining friendships outside of her fellow educators at work because she was either there or at home. Mom's "escape" or downtime was grocery shopping or her weekly trip to Walmart. The impeccably kept house has become a maze of pathways amongst the stack of stuff from what has now been years of significant hoarding. There is not a flat surface left in my childhood home that isn't piled high with something or other. The two musketeers don't see that her trying to be the mom and wife who tried desperately to be and do everything for everyone else cost her her own health, mental and otherwise. That the years of looking for answers and trying to get help for those she loved most left her feeling alone and bothersome more than anything else. I've shared with her many times how terrified I am that my pursuit of raising a good human, no matter what, could potentially cost me the same. By not accepting the "he'll grow out of it" answers given about boys with behavioral challenges or impulse control issues. By insisting on counseling and medication to help support AJ to be his best self could make him resent me and gravitate to others who he perceives are easier on him. I'm extremely grateful that my son's father, his current wife, and I can now put AJ first. I was only recently able to meet his wife after years of that being prevented for whatever reason. I thanked her from the bottom of my heart for all she does for AJ when he's over there. How much I appreciate her and her patience and the tough expectations she puts on him. She said she knows how difficult it is to do it alone when I have him and she understands that because of navigating that with her own three children. *She said she knows it takes a village and it's impossible to do alone.* What a gift! We have gotten to a place where it's three against one. No more of AJ dividing and conquering, pitting us against each other with his obvious but often effective manipulations. I think about the three of us as a united front at this point, and we're divorced, for crying out loud!

My folks have always been together, but there was never a united front when it came to tough love and holding us accountable as kids. Dad came home at night after rehearsals to a clean and calm home and couldn't understand why Mom was a raving lunatic when all was so peaceful now. Well, she'd just been through WWIII trying to help us with our homework and get dinner cooked and served, the kitchen cleaned, the lunches packed, and baths given, all with intermittent screaming fits and hateful things spewed at her by a little boy who likely needed medication and therapy all along. Unfortunately, my dad did not believe in either tool. I remember us all going to ONE family counseling session when we were kids. The counselor asked what brought us in and how she could help, and I can still hear my dad say, "I don't know because I don't even understand what we're doing here." That was our one and only visit to group family therapy. We went to Luby's cafeteria to eat lunch on the way home and that was the end of that. I've realized that Dad is essentially conflict averse on the home front, leaving mom standing alone in dealing with things that should've been dealt with as a team. The two of them together. A united front. The relationship between my father and my brother has always been more that of a friendship than that of a parent and a child. No accountability. Lots of enabling and placating that left my mom standing alone as the bad guy in the situation. Eventually, I feel that she gave up and part of her obsession with assisting AJ was her attempt at a do-over, and the hoarding in the house?? In my mind almost a "Fuck You" to my father and brother. That was the one thing she could do and have control over, and so she did.

My mother has taught me so much in life. I call it "Mom's suitcase," filled with so many tidbits of wisdom over the years. Lessons from her own trials and tribulations. She'd say to me that the lessons I get to learn on this journey go into my suitcase of life. I can share these lessons with others so they may learn from my mistakes and experiences. This is the main reason for me wanting to write this book.

However, I don't want you to see it as "emotional baggage" in your mind when you picture it. I want to be sure I differentiate the idea of this life suitcase of experience from emotional baggage or a *"griefcase,"* if you will. I hope that, perhaps, for someone reading this book, the information here might serve as their own survival guide. A survival guide that might help you negotiate and deal with the life lessons, experiences, and traumas that you carry in your own suitcase of life. When you decide to do the work to heal from whatever trauma you've had to deal with in your life, you're not healing so you can better handle the after-effects of the trauma. You're used to having to deal with the shitty bits of life. You're healing so you can learn how to truly accept and invite joy into your life. Let me share a bit of wisdom I've learned from my years as a woman in the corporate world: you don't get what you deserve; you get what you negotiate.

Your own suitcase should be filled with lessons and experiences for you to learn from so you can continuously improve not only to become your best self but to also learn to accept the ugliest parts of yourself exactly as they are. Those "ugly" parts are just as important to identify and own as they too make up what is holistically and wonderfully you!

My mom has always said to me: "*You remember who you are, Catherine Alexander Trimble! Honor her and be great!*" She'd also often say, "*chin up and chest out, Missy!*" Now I doubt she ever imagined I'd translate that to "Tits Up", or publish a book titled what this one is, but I'm doing my damndest to be authentically me and the best me I can be! Even with the ugly parts.

I've learned some tough lessons along the way that have made their way into my own suitcase. "*Let them*" was an important lesson for me to learn. I think so many of us go through life worrying about what others think about us, say about us, and tell others about us. To the point of dysfunction at times. This lesson helped me learn that holding onto resentment or entertaining the thought of revenge that pops into your mind won't help at all. It's like this definition of anger I read somewhere once that said, "Anger is a punishment you give yourself for someone else's mistake." That hit hard! Because it's so true. You're upsetting yourself when you get angry at something someone else did. You're allowing your blood pressure to rise and for your emotions to get dysregulated while the other person just carries on with their life. Anger is probably the least helpful and most destructive of emotions if we don't work through it and just hold onto it instead. Fear a close second, maybe.

So let them. Let them talk about you. Let them throw stones. Let them make their own mistakes. Let them think whatever they want to think. It's none of your business anyway. When you have a healthy sense of self and self-worth, what others think and say about you just doesn't bother you anymore. And boy, is it liberating!

Another gold nugget from Mom's suitcase is her telling me to "*expect nothing, but be prepared for joy.*" I think it kind of ties in with the idea of detachment theory, which basically teaches you not to attach yourself to certain expected outcomes because it inevitably leads to disappointment. This immediately brings to mind the idea of manifesting and how people get it wrong. You may think that this goes against the idea of expecting good things to happen in your life. There's a difference between expecting and accepting. Accept whatever it is. When you accept reality for what it is at any given moment, there can be no pain, resentment, anger, or misery. True acceptance is the key to contentment. If you want to change something and you can change it, change it. Otherwise, just accept it for what it is.

It's easier said than done, I know. It's because we're programmed to react. Ask yourself when and who taught you how to pay attention to and regulate whatever is happening inside you at any given moment in your life. Has anyone ever taught you how to do that? Have you taught yourself? Only when we are in control of our inner world can the outer world no longer influence it to such a high degree.

So, I urge you to train yourself to practice acceptance in your life. Learn to look for the "glimmers" on a daily basis. We're so used to looking out for and reacting to the triggers that surround us that we forget to look out for and be grateful for the glimmers or moments of joy in our lives. Savor the moments that bring you joy, happiness, laughter, peace, and gratitude.

Consider what you want to fill your own suitcase with. Are you content with life just randomly happening to you? Or do you want to take charge and create the life you've always wanted? Learn how to do the things you struggle with and place those lessons in your suitcase of life so you can pull it out whenever you need, reminding you that you have whatever you need to overcome any obstacle that life throws at you. And if you cannot find it in your suitcase, I can guarantee that someone else out there has it in theirs. You can find it online in YouTube videos, online courses, books, podcasts, talks, etc.

We all have suitcases filled with wisdom. The purpose of life is to share what you've learned with others so they may teach the next person, and so on. Hence the level of vulnerability and authenticity I hope you find in this book. No more, only including what looks good! Just real, good/bad/ugly REALNESS!

Life is short and finite; nothing here is yours to keep. When you go, you don't get to take anything with you. Share what's in your suitcase and learn from what is in others.

Chapter 16

Tuck in Your Shirt and Fuck the Rest

Marked Safe From

Giving AF
Today

I think it is absolutely CRAZY just how much of our self-esteem gets all wrapped up in social norms. Don't you think it's crazy to allow what someone else thinks to influence you in a way that leads so many millions of girls who grow into women who feel absolutely insecure in their own beautiful bodies with their unique talents and skills? I think it's absolutely ridiculous.

Don't get me wrong, I've allowed myself to get all wrapped up in that bullshit before. Feeling bad about what I see in the mirror. I mean, who hasn't? Hence the title of this chapter! I've always been on the heavier side, now referred to as thicker, and I love that! I'm not heavy, assholes; I'm thick! I'll never have a bikini body, and I don't know if I'd wear one if I did, as I'm kinda private that way, but I always wished I could tuck in a blouse and rock a cute belt! I did what I needed to do for ME to feel confident and comfortable in my own skin, and now I do tuck that shit in! Best feeling ever! Take it or leave it; this is me! Unless you suffer from narcissistic personality disorder, you've probably been there too. We see all these beautiful size zero models with flawless skin, perky boobs, and a thigh gap on the cover of magazines and Instagram channels and think to ourselves, "Man, I wish I looked like that." You shop for cute panties, and for anyone without the thigh gap and size zero body described above as the societal preference, you have to pick whether you prefer both lips or both cheeks covered because those panties aren't gonna do both. There's nothing wrong with wanting to improve yourself, of course. It just depends on where that need or motivation comes from. Is it coming from a place of low self-esteem or from a place of recognizing that something needs changing to improve your health? If it's the latter, it's all good.

Your body is uniquely yours, and as hard as it may be to accept, what others think about it is their problem. If you're overweight and want to lose weight for your health, that's great. But if you do it because you cringe at the looks other people give you or because you feel like you're not good enough because of the quips from passersby, then we have a problem. Some may think it is a valid motivation. I don't. It's unhealthy, and unless you're doing it for the right reasons, you'll land right back where you started before you can say *fad diets*.

I feel like healthy self-esteem is one of the rarest things on this planet, mainly because we too easily judge one another. And I think we do it because it's so much easier to throw stones at others than to look at ourselves in the mirror and recognize what needs changing to make us better, healthier, more secure human beings. It's easier to leave nasty comments on someone's social media posts than to use that time to improve yourself.

People who are secure within themselves don't break others down. It just goes to show how many insecure people there are in the world if you look at social media and all the nasty comments flying around. It's like people don't have anything better to do with their lives. A secure person won't look you up and down when you enter a room and give you unsolicited feedback on what needs changing. No one fucking asked you, Karen, so just shut up and focus on yourself.

We also give men way too much power in affecting our self-esteem. Like that piece of work that tells you that you have a pretty face but would be much prettier if you lost a few. Or the guy who, after you do lose the weight, tells you that you may look good to guys with your clothes on but wait until they see you naked. Seriously? He can fuck all the way off to the top of fuck off mountain and then fuck off a lot more! How about the guy who says, "Your boobs look a bit saggy without a bra." Yeah, well, your dick looks minuscule without an erection and that's not happening either. So, what's your point? What do men even find attractive about boobs anyway? They're literally just some balls of fat on a woman's chest. If you can love that bit of fat, why can't you love the fat on my stomach?

We really invest too much in others' opinions. Girl, if you want the boob job or the tummy tuck, do it! It's none of anyone's business, and if it's going to make you feel better about yourself, do it. You can accept and love yourself while also treating yourself to what you want to look better for yourself. Not for others. For YOU! I like putting on makeup now and again. I like how it makes me feel. Not what others think of it. How it makes ME feel.

Don't like the saggy skin? Have it removed! Not a fan of your nipples lining up with your belly button, get those suckers lifted! Tired of the saggy, full diaper look in your pants? Kardashian the shit out of that ass! Wrinkles? Do the Botox or filler. But please be careful with the filler! It's one thing to treat your "what the fuck" lines between your brows and not have much facial expression ability left. It's a whole other thing to look nothing like yourself and have your face ID on your cell phone stop working!

As previously mentioned, I'm a big Mel Robbins fan, and one of my favorite things from her I've put into practice is the "mirror-facing self high-five" daily. To look in the mirror and tell myself, "*Okay, sis. You've got this!*"

You need to learn to be your biggest cheerleader because no one can do it like you. No one is coming to save you. No one can do the work for you. And it's no one's responsibility but your own.

I had recently been invited to a friend's home for a get-together to celebrate their new patio area. They're a couple that I admire greatly and have always been very kind and supportive of me. I wasn't feeling it because of a lot going on at that time that was really heavy on my heart. I was wearing black leggings, my maroon, perfectly imperfect sweatshirt, and had my hair in a ponytail under a baseball cap. No makeup whatsoever. I ran to water some plants at the house of a recently deceased mother of a friend of mine who no longer lives in town. Driving there, I felt bad about saying I'd stop by the party and not doing so, so I pulled an audible and went. Allie in her baseball cap and leggings without a drop of makeup. I wouldn't have done that for a million bucks in the past, and although I apologized for my attire and lack of makeup, I showed up. Not for them, as they'd have noticed, but it wouldn't have been a big deal. I did it for me! And it felt great to chat and enjoy a glass of wine and some good conversation and not to give a rat's ass about what anyone might have thought about how I looked that afternoon.

Or how about the swim party I recently, and willingly, attended?! I'm sorry, a swim party? For adults? Ummm who is the sadistic asshole that decided this would be fun? In the past, I would have come up with some excuse to avoid going. Or at the very best, I'd have shown up fully clothed and stated that I couldn't stay long enough to get in the water, so I didn't bring a suit. Allie 2.0?? This Allie?? She showed up in shorts and all her pasty white glory with a swimsuit in tow! Cellulite on my thick ass and thighs? Check. 100 SPF? Check. Laughs with college friends to last a lifetime? Check.

I realized I'd hit an all-time high on the concept of accepting myself the way I am not too long ago. This may be TMI (too much information), but if not 100% vulnerable, then what's the point, right? I had been dating someone for a bit, and we had our first night together. No, Karen, we're not married and judge away, but we are two consenting adults. And for those of you wondering but too afraid to ask, his plumbing worked perfectly! Hallelujah! I've always been the lights off, under three blankets kind of gal, so I was astonished when I found myself walking through his house in all my naked glory to get us some recovery water to drink. I jokingly hollered that I sure hoped there weren't cameras in his house as I walked through the living room and kitchen in my birthday suit. I burst out laughing when he yelled back from his bedroom, "*Feel free to put on my flip-flops.*" I stood in the kitchen getting us water, thinking, "Who is this person?" Not him. ME! Who is this 4o something-year-old woman so comfortable in her own skin that she's being intimate with some low lighting, on top of the covers, and now walking through someone else's house completely naked? Allie and her growing self-esteem for the win!

Your job on this planet is to be as authentically you as you can possibly be. There's no one else like you. Do you know what the odds are of you being alive? Four hundred trillion to one! One in a million doesn't even scratch the surface! You were meant to be here. You were meant to live this life. And seeing as life is so short (because it could end at any moment), don't you think it is time that you live however the fuck you see fit? If your confidence intimidates someone else, that's totally their problem to deal with. #ftp (fuck them people). You didn't come here to play small. Perhaps you just don't remember who the fuck you are. You are one of the very, very few people who get to live this life on Earth as a human being. You might be thinking, "Few? Hah! There are eight billion people on this planet!" Sure, but do you know how small that number is compared to how many people could possibly be alive? It doesn't even register on the Universal scale. Stop investing your precious energy into what others think of you. Surround yourself with a forcefield of flying fucks. Or if you're a little less trucker/sailor in your colorful vocabulary, your own personal sparkle bubble as my friend Laura says. No one can break through that! Personally however, I prefer to repeat the daily affirmation of "I embrace my inner badass and give zero fucks what other people think" from my favorite yoga master…Yoga Bryan! Look him up! Namasté mothafucka. Sometimes, one middle finger just isn't enough. That's why you have two. AJ says it isn't a coincidence that my middle fingernails are usually the first to be broken or missing. He really is my kid, that's for sure.

This life we get to live is an immensely precious experience. I think that if we were to do the research, it would show that a shockingly small number of people truly appreciate the fact that life is so special and fleeting at the same time. It's like when you see something new for the first time. Let's say someone's never seen the ocean before, and they get to visit a beach. It's amazing and magical all at once! But let's say that person now moves to an ocean-side villa and gets to see the ocean every day. What do you think happens a year later? Those sparks of amazement will have faded away, and they will take it for granted. Meh, it's just the ocean. Meh, it's just life.

Yes, it is life. And it can end today. You don't know. No one does. So, learn to appreciate this gift that is life and the fact that you get to live it.

Learn to appreciate every little bit of it, every single day that you are lucky enough to breathe in the air.

I've learned to be grateful for the wrinkles, the gray hair, and even the scars. I've laughed, cried, struggled, triumphed, failed, worried, been hurt, and SURVIVED to earn them! Many people would've done anything for that opportunity. The opportunity to still be looking down at the dirt! For just one more day to make your mark.

I know, as a woman, I'm supposed to be afraid of getting older, but I love this shit so much! Every year, I sink deeper into this bath of unapologetic realness, and it's amazing! It's so liberating. I was texting with a friend last week who shared that she wished she'd known then some of what she knows now. I shared with her how I feel like we all need to live until about 50 for the knowledge and life lessons and then get a do-over! Start again, but WITH that 50yrs of accumulated knowledge. Now THAT would be a game changer! Do you know what most women secretly wish for? That they could just be themselves. So, if you have that ability, hold onto it with all you have. You have reached a ninja level of acceptance that few ever will. If nothing else, celebrate yourself for that because it is a major accomplishment.

Isn't it ridiculous that the simple act of allowing ourselves to just be unapologetically us should be something we celebrate because it's so rare? It's bonkers. But it's also the reality we have to deal with.

This life can truly fuck with you. Unfuck yourself. You cannot be who you were before all the things that happened that dulled your fucking shine. BUT you must learn to shine again in your own light with all the experiences and lessons learned providing even more wattage! Shine bright like a diamond. You know that diamonds are formed under immense pressure. So, when you find yourself under immense pressure, just remember that you're going through the process of becoming a diamond.

If you find that you don't have big-girl panties big enough for the job, put on your kick-ass boots and go commando. We all get sick of underwear and responsibilities sometimes, right? Do whatever you can to feel comfortable and confident in your skin.

So, whenever you feel like you're not good enough, or whenever someone makes you feel this way – tuck in your shirt and fuck the rest! I guarantee you that when you are able to do this, the women looking on secretly admire and are likely even a bit jealous of you. Strut your stuff, bish.

Chapter 17

Burnt Toast

Don't you just find life's little mishaps to be super annoying?

Like when you accidentally burn the toast, and it causes you to be a few minutes late.

Or when you forget something and need to get out of the car and run back into the house. Or when your son's leaky diaper spills a bladder full of warm urine into a puddle in your lap at Easter Sunday church service, forcing you to hold him cradled in the waist of your dress to prevent all that golden liquid from inadvertently baptizing some poor soul as you crawl across the people in your pew, exiting stage left of the sanctuary in church. Or when you're stuck in a meeting and know you'll be late for supper. Or when you're in a rush and run into chatty Kathy, who you know there's no escaping, so it causes you to miss your bus.

Where am I going with this? Well, it kind of circles back to the idea of total acceptance.

Maybe you burned the toast, and it causing you to be five minutes late, just prevented you from being in the accident that happened just five minutes ago on your regular route to work. Maybe the lap full of liquid gold happened because someone you really didn't want to run into would be in your communion line. Maybe you are stuck in that meeting because someone in that meeting will see your potential and help advance your career. Or maybe you ran into chatty Kathy because the bus you were supposed to be on, but missed, now has Sandra Bullock and Keanu Reeves on it, trying not to have it explode by slowing down because some douchebag strapped a bomb to it. If you don't know what I'm talking about, I'm giving away my age.

I know "Everything happens for a reason" is such a cliche, but I really do believe it. I believe this is the school of life; we all have to walk our paths and learn our own lessons. But, in the end, the Universe always has your back. You just need to have faith and accept that whatever comes your way is always meant for you. It's the same as saying, *"God doesn't give you more than you can carry."* Whatever is meant for you will always find you and stay. What isn't will evade you or leave. You have to be open to the loss and keep putting one foot in front of the other because you just never know what amazing experience or opportunity is waiting for you right around the corner. And I don't know about you, but I refuse to be the quitter that throws their arms up in surrender and quits just before the breakthrough!

Be grateful for closed doors, bad vibes, and stuff that falls apart. It's divine protection from people, places, and things that no longer align with your soul and purpose. I was convinced to apply for a promotion I wasn't sure I wanted because if I couldn't change things for the better, then who? I went through three interviews, and in the final one, I was asked my thoughts on something and made the conscious decision at the moment to be honest in my feedback, knowing it would cost me the promotion. I got a call later that week from my boss at the time. I was told, "I hope you're happy because, after all you shared, clearly you will not be getting the job," followed by an email cc'ing the CEO saying she "regretted to inform me that a decision was made to go in a different direction and that she hoped I could accept that and take the weekend to make peace with their decision." I replied there was no peace to be made, that I firmly believed some doors were better off closed, and that this was simply not a door that was meant for me. Have a great weekend! And I meant it.

This promotion would have required a fair amount of travel. About a month after that ordeal, my custody situation changed. My son's father said he had a lot going on and needed a break and some downtime, and he would only be taking our son for about half the time each month that he had been when I'd thrown my hat in the ring. One month after that, Dad was diagnosed with terminal cancer, and we started traveling for treatment at MD Anderson in Houston every three weeks. What would I have done if that particular door had been opened for me? Thank you for the burnt toast, Universe!

The point is, you just never know. We get so wrapped up in our problems that we forget to see all the blessings we take for granted. Yes, maybe something you really wanted didn't work out, and maybe you feel really pissed off about it. But *MAYBE* it didn't work out for a reason. *MAYBE* it would've been a horrible mistake.

I know that I've had times when I've looked up at the sky and asked, "Why?" Times when I've cried my eyes out, feeling like there's just no point in continuing to try so damn hard. But when I look back now, it makes sense. They say hindsight is 20/20 because it's true. This is how cliches get to become cliches. Because it's a fundamental truth learned and repeated by many people worldwide until it becomes a cliche.

Yes, it might suck the big one at the moment, but often, when you look back, you're able to go, "Ohhh, that's why!" Not everyone has the ability to do that, most often because they don't want to. It's so much easier to place blame elsewhere than accept responsibility for whatever reality you've created for yourself.

Granted, there's so much that is outside of our control. Stop focusing on that. What's the use of trying to control what is outside of your control? It's a one-way ticket to Misery Island, my friend. I know because I've visited that island more times in my life than I care to admit. It sucks there. Do you know what else I learned in the process? It's a CHOICE!!

You have way more control than you think you have. We just CHOOSE to ignore it because it's easier to find fault elsewhere or blame someone or something else rather than take a long, hard look in the mirror. It IS hard! I know. But it is also the most important and fulfilling work anyone can do for themselves. When you are able to take control of yourself, your choices, your thoughts, and your behaviors let me tell you, you become a force to be reckoned with. This is when you can start seeing the many blessings in disguise that surround you.

That guy who broke your heart when he slept with your best friend? The Universe did that to protect you. You chose not to see the red flags because you thought he and your bestie would never destroy both relationships in that manner. Maybe the Universe brought the two of them together to show you that you are wasting your time on people who are not worth it. Two hoes, one stone, or however the saying goes.

Every single person who crosses your path has a lesson to teach you. The question is, how often are you aware of and searching out the lesson to be learned? Don't get me wrong. This is a journey, and it can be messy. I admit I have looked up at the sky and yelled 'I don't want this lesson! I don't want to learn this one!' more times than I'd care to admit. But I've learned them. Sadly, some more than once. Some people come into our lives for a season. Others stay for a few seasons. Very few are there throughout your life. The person you'll spend the most time with is you! You are a blessing. You are the one worth fighting for. You are the bee's knees, baby!

So, stop allowing others to treat you as anything less than a miracle. Stop chasing what's not for you. Stop trying to control what you can't. Start focusing on the blessings in your life. Don't take that shit for granted. There is so much learning, living, and growth to do that you shouldn't waste your time with anything but what is good for you. In fact, from this moment going forward, I want you to make a promise to yourself that you are going to focus more on seeing the blessings that surround you every single day, even if it's just a tiny cloud in the sky that looks like Karen's saggy tits that made you chuckle for a moment.

The Universe truly has your back. But understand this: it doesn't care about your intentions. You can have all the best intentions in the world. The Universe applauds action, not intention. It will back you up, but you have to do the rest of the work. You have to make yourself aware of the unhelpful behaviors you've adopted that need changing. I have someone I care deeply for in my life who has repeatedly said I'm in church praying for forgiveness or I'm headed to church praying for resolution to a situation. I've often wanted to remind him of that joke where the guy gets to the pearly gates and says I've prayed and asked you to save me from the drowning waters over and over and now here I am, dead. God responds that he sent a rowboat, then a motorboat, and finally a helicopter, all with people to save him and reminds him that he declined them all. We can pray until we're purple, but you have to act on the intention. Not just pray on it and hope it changes. Sticking our head in the sand and hoping things will get better does nothing to actually improve the situation, no matter how many prayers are said, or positive intentions are held. You have the responsibility to CHOOSE which thoughts you allow yourself to focus on on a daily basis. You may not control the emotions that come up at any given moment, but what you do control is what you do about it. Feeling anger rising inside of you? Choose to remind yourself of the definition of anger, engage in some grounding tools, and "hoosaaa" your way out of that shit. It's not helpful, and it's not for you. Everything you cannot control is there for a reason. You just focus on what is within your control and let the Universe take care of the rest.

Everything happens for a reason.

Yes, Karen, even that burnt toast! So I say burn, baby burn!

Chapter 18

Jesus, Take the Wheel

I struggle with the whole concept of "Let go and let God." I do take comfort in the idea that there's some master puppeteer up in the clouds that has all this shit under control and planned out. I think. I hope. I pray?

One of my favorite all-time memes is the one that says, "Jesus, take the wheel." It shows an old-fashioned vehicle on a dirt road with a wheel coming off and flying into the brush with the driver yelling, "Jesus! Not that wheel!" This visually describes my struggle to know what I want and pray for, may not be part of God's plan.

I've struggled with the concept of organized religion for years. I grew up attending whatever church Dad or his brass quintet was playing for at the time. To that degree, I've been Methodist (baptized there), Baptist, Presbyterian, and Episcopalian. I've had Catholics say they're catholic and not Christian. Um, how's that, exactly? Lots of Jewish friends growing up and as an adult, as well as Jehovah's Witnesses and Mormons. To that same point, I have agnostic and atheist friends, as well as those that believe in the universe itself as some sort of higher power. I love and respect them all the same as they do me. The divisiveness occurring as a result of differing religious viewpoints is appalling to me.

I look around the world and current events with Israel under attack. The Gaza strip all but blown to smithereens. With terrorist attacks becoming more and more frequent all over the world. So much hatred. So much violence. Some individuals killing and torturing innocent people in the name of their God. I can't imagine any God wanting the torture, heartbreak, and death we are becoming desensitized to. We grow up with it and see it on TV every day. I can't imagine any God wanting the casualties of war in their name.

Political parties, politicians, and judges who make life and death HEALTHCARE decisions for women while proclaiming religion and God's will as the reason. Women becoming septic and dying with trained healthcare professionals and physicians staring on, helpless to intercede because she happens to live in a state that prohibits abortion (while taking away a woman's rights), and anyone who participates will be fined to high heaven and/or lose their licensure, and with that, their ability to provide for their own families. Or they might even be sent to jail.

So, let me get this straight. We're to believe that God wants the 31-year-old, who's wanted nothing more than to be a mom, to lose her ability to try again or to possibly lose her own life when the fetus she and her husband wanted so desperately, and she has been carrying, is found to have no brain or that its organs are growing outside of its body. Or the woman who was raped and become pregnant as a result who has made the incredibly difficult decision to abort, isn't allowed to? I'm sorry, but in what world does that make sense? Don't get me wrong, I don't believe in abortion as a form of repetitive birth control, but I do believe that any God would be troubled by where things are today and by the fact that some of these politicians proclaim it's in his name.

With the upcoming US Presidential election, there are incredibly high stakes, and watching the recent political national committees, it seems the divisiveness is at an all time high in this broken and intrinsically flawed two party system. To watch the recent debate, you'd have thought you were watching a scene from Grumpy Old Men! Two grown ass men on the national stage contending for the opportunity to represent our UNITED States, fighting like teenagers. Teaching our kids that name calling and bullying others is fair game? How on earth do we vote in good conscience for individuals to represent our country on the international stage when they are essentially brawling for all to see on our own? Without term limits preventing career politicians from being in office up until they literally die, I'm concerned the voting general public no longer has the power of the people as originally intended. We have folks having transient ischemic attacks live on camera still in office. Others who are rolled in and propped up to vote that pass away hours later. By any chance did y'all watch the series Designated Survivor with Keifer Sutherland? I've said to a handful of people that short of a complete reboot, which by the way our representatives would have to vote for themselves, I don't know what the future holds for this great nation or the children in it. We seem some days to be on the brink of a nuclear WWIII and other days a Christian Nationalist civil war. Now let me be clear, I am by NO MEANS suggesting we blow up the capital as in the premise of the show, however without a massive overhaul, God help us all.

Sadly, I often think that "God" and religion are used as a shield for people to hide behind while judging and condemning others. I can't imagine a God wanting an entire group of people or an entire demographic made to feel lesser than or unworthy in any way. I have many gay friends who are incredibly spiritual and grapple with this topic, often having been quoted verses in the Bible telling them that who and what they are is wrong. The God I know and love expects the final judgment of all of us to be left to him. Not the person who breaks your heart by mailing you a letter filled with unsolicited judgment, telling you how disappointed she is that you've lost your way and are living in sin because you are living with a man to whom you are yet to be married. Not the person who tells you that you are letting down both your son and God by not being in church every week. Not the person who tells you while your heart is broken, and you've been made to feel like an outsider in your own family that God wants you to forgive and forget. That you need to be a good Christian and just let it go and simply love those who have hurt you. All the while refusing to acknowledge how we got to this point in the first place, let alone lift a finger to help change it.

Money and the church have always been a sore subject for me. It's like a pay-to-play scenario in my mind. Making offerings when able and called to do so is one thing. Feeling as though (and being told essentially) that securing your place, being a valued member, or establishing your name and place in the church requires tithing just rubs me the wrong way. So, I can be a terrible person or commit horrible acts, but if I repent and tithe 10% of my income, we're good? I have the Willy Wonka golden ticket, then? I don't think so.

I know a lot of people who lead lives I'd be proud of. They donate and give of themselves their entire lives. They support amazing causes and work diligently to make the world a better place. They are true pillars of society and give limitless support. That are true believers doing the work.

Are you saying they're doomed if they don't sit in a pew every Sunday and don't tithe to the church? But that the person next to them who is cheating on their partner or spouse, had or requested their partner have an abortion, has broken an endless list of hearts with their behavior, but is sitting there bright and shiny each Sunday and tithing their fair share is all good? If that's the case, I'm gonna need me some s'mores fix-ins for the pits of hell downstairs!

I was always the person they teased and thanked for her presence in church during services on Easter and Christmas etc. Mostly because I loved the chance to hear the organ music. Listening to my father and the El Paso brass quintet play the hallelujah chorus is something straight from heaven. I give of myself to those I know need me. The people who need some financial help. Those who need my love or attention or ear or shoulder or guidance. I talk to God and the universe regularly. I pray regularly. I consider myself a faithful person, but it doesn't matter to those who judge me for not sitting in a pew in my Sunday best.

I remember when I was a practicing nurse on call for trauma and the cardiac cath lab, I'd pray the whole way in from my car each time for my hands to bring healing and peace to my patient. To help and never hurt. To do no harm. I'd ask God to please help me help them and help me to not make a mistake that would cause their situation to be any more challenging than it already was.

As a mother, I pray a lot, mostly for him to help me not totally lose my mind while trying to raise this amazing boy he has loaned me. To not fail my son and let my hurt or pain ever impact him, but to also heed the painful lessons I've learned so as to protect him from the same. To always protect him to the best of my ability both physically, mentally, and emotionally. I pray for God to guide me in his ways to help me raise a good human. A wonderful man to eventually be a great husband and father should that be the path he chooses. I pray all the time for my dad to stay pain-free and asymptomatic to the end of his battle against terminal cancer. I pray for peace in my mom's mind and heart after so many years of hurt. I pray for calm and happiness for my brother. I pray for health, safety, and abundance for my sister and her family. (I have a half-sister from my father's first marriage who I've unfortunately not had the opportunity to get to know as well due to us living far apart) I pray for peace for myself and for people to just allow me to live my life on my terms. I pray for God to help me continue working on myself to be the best mama, friend, daughter, sister, boss, coworker, and overall human I can be.

I believe in a higher power and do my best to live a life I feel he'd be accepting, if not proud of. If not tithing or sitting in a church pew every week costs me a place in heaven, then what a disappointment. I mentioned earlier that if that's how it is, I'd need some s'mores for downstairs. I've often over the years told dear friends as we laughed at some dark humor or cussed up a storm or drank too much or said too much that I'd see them in hell, but not to worry because I'd bring the marshmallows so we can roast them for s'mores while we sit around sweating in the flames. This menopause shit is rough so the idea of an eternity of that is sure as hell not appealing! I genuinely hope that by leading my best life and giving of myself, keeping an open dialogue with and asking for forgiveness when I inevitably screw something up, somehow, my good will outweigh my shortcomings, and instead, I'll find myself reunited with all my fur babies, family, and friends and make that ultimate final cut.

What I don't subscribe to is the idea that completely hypocritical jerks who live ugly lives and hurt people wherever they go will somehow be guaranteed a space because their butt's in a pew each week as a tithing member to some church. When we discuss it, Royal Flush often compares it to how the drug dealers and major gang leaders often give massive amounts of money to their neighborhood clergy. Yeah some for protection etc, but many out of some misguided attempt to make up for their lifelong atrocities. An extreme example perhaps, but the same if you really think about it.

My choices regarding this area of my life have caused some friction for me in certain relationships. The assumption made that my choice not to tithe or consistently attend Sunday services somehow translates to a lack of faith or relationship with my God and that it must mean I'm not a believer. I have, at times in my life, struggled with my beliefs. I've asked myself the questions about if there really is a God, a higher power, a master puppeteer in the sky, then why? Why the illness and death and evil and war and heartache and loss? But I also believe in my heart that this cannot be it. The proverbial rat race of life cannot be the ultimate destination. I talk to God all the time. Sometimes on the floor when brought to my knees by some event or circumstance. Sometimes, while driving to pick AJ up from school, I pray that he had a good day at school and not been bullied or hurt, as it always results in him getting in the car in tears. I also ask for help and guidance in supporting him through these types of struggles in life. Kids can be so mean to one another. It breaks my heart to see my boy in pain.

Sometimes, sitting in the waiting room at MD Anderson, I pray that Dad's treatment goes well and beg for good results partially because I cannot fathom having to be the one to call the family and share bad news. Sometimes, before a big meeting or an important conversation, I ask Him to help me find the right words at the right time and to help my audience have an open mind and truly understand the position from which I come. Sometimes, when we're lying in bed at night, yes, my 12-year-old sleeps with me, Karen. He moved in when his father moved out, saying no one else was sleeping there, so why not him? Who could argue with that...six years later! I'll treasure keeping him as close to me as possible for as long as he allows me. His legs draped over the top of mine, and his sweet, still, childlike voice says, "Goodnight, mama. I love you more." I simply thank God for this life I'm living with this precious boy he has gifted me.

To me, my "religion" is love. It's faith. It's praying when times are good and bad and having a regular dialogue with the universe. It is being the best person I can be and living my life in a way I can always look myself in the mirror and be proud of the person looking back at me. It's being good to those I come in contact with and honoring Him through my actions, not just words, donations, and pictures in front of a church posted on social media. It is me living my best authentic life in front of God and everyone else in the most loving way possible.

BUDDHA was not a BUDDHIST. JESUS was not a CHRISTIAN. MUHAMMAD was not a MUSLIM. THEY were TEACHERS who taught LOVE. LOVE was their RELIGION. So, I learn from these amazing teachers and adapt THEIR religion as mine. LOVE.

Love is the ultimate religion. Imagine if we all taught ourselves how to love and accept one another completely. Hell, what if we learned to simply accept OURSELVES completely? How different the world would be. And the kicker is, there's absolutely no reason not to.

Chapter 19

#procaffeinator - Maybe She's Born With It, Maybe It's Caffeine

This chapter is all about my love affair with coffee. At one point, a friend told me that they'd decided that perhaps I had it all wrong. That instead of me being addicted to coffee, perhaps coffee is addicted to me! She's a brilliant friend of mine, and I mean it's possible! Afterall, I do have quite the magnetic personality. I do love me a good cuppa Joe. Side bar...do you know where the phrase "cup of Joe" originated? I was on a trip to NYC several years ago and sat down to get my java on in a really neat eclectic coffee house. There was a story on the menu that I looked into and it goes something like this. Back in the day, the Navy was known as the party branch of the military as the liquor apparently flowed freely aboard the ships and the recruits were known to be pretty rowdy. Secretary of the

Navy "Joe" Daniel, banned alcohol on all ships in 1914, leaving the sailors with nothing more than coffee to pass the time. They called it a "cup of Joe" as a dig at the gentlemen who made the change. A coffee company in NYC ran an advertising campaign with the phrase as their marketing ploy and it was so successful they later trademarked it. Anywho...not many things can top that first sip of coffee hitting your tongue first thing in the morning. Man, it's good! The best part of it is the sound of no one talking to me while I get my Java on. Unless this Java is being delivered in bed by some knight in no armor, I'd find that acceptable. Still no talking, though. Otherwise, I'll have to whip out my "leave me the fa-cologne" while I take solace in that mug until I'm ready to take on the world. And yet again this morning, no naked knight stood next to my bed saying, *"Good morning, Your Royal Highness, here is your cup of coffee."* So disappointing.

Coffee is the main thing that keeps me going until it's socially acceptable to drink alcohol. Don't you judge me, Karen. The caffeine in that Java in your hand is technically a psychoactive drug. We all have our own coping mechanisms to help us make it through the day. All I know is my birthstone is a coffee bean, and instead of blood, you'll find coffee running through my veins. I don't cry over spilled milk, but I will cry like a kid whose ice cream just slipped off the cone and fell on the floor over spilled coffee, that's for sure. It's a magical drug, caffeine. It even creates this illusion that I have my shit together from time to time. I don't. But it's nice to feel like I do. Even if it's just for a little while. Another great thing about coffee is that it keeps me from biting people, which I've been told is socially unacceptable. Between cocaine and coffee, it seems like the whole point of Colombia is to wake the rest of the world up. I'd probably be doing 25 to life in some women's prison now if it wasn't for coffee. And as we've established by now, orange is not my color.

Batman has the bat signal. Me? A coffee bean-shaped light shining against the sky. And just in case you were wondering, Karen, I do not know how many cups of coffee it takes to be friendly. But I do know for a fact that it's not eight.

Coffee and I had a love-hate relationship for a bit after I had an incident that involved it on a business trip. I'd been up all night working on a presentation about why we shouldn't rebrand the urgent care centers I oversaw to a national brand. To say my opinion wasn't popular was an understatement, and I knew it was going to be a tough crowd. I had a single K-cup brewer I traveled with because I've heard horror stories about things found in those nasty little single-brew coffee machines provided by hotels. Thanks a lot for that one, "Greece". I set up my travel mug perfectly, with just the right amount of creamer, sweetener, and protein powder. Picked out my H-E-B San Antonio flavored K-cup from the assortment in my suitcase, filled the brewer with water, and hit go. I turned around, leaning back on the counter with the magic happening just behind me. You know, the one where these ugly ground-up beans get washed with hot water and produce this magical potion of life? As I stood there reviewing my pitch in my head and possible questions I might get, I suddenly had a major hot flash. Except only my butt was hot. In my overthinking and over-preparing state, I'd prepared everything perfectly but neglected to put the mug under the Keurig dispenser! I'd stood there thinking positively and literally manifested a hot ass! As in a scalding, unbearably hot ass, which wasn't quite what I had in mind. Luckily for me, I hadn't put my dress on yet, so my wardrobe change only required different big girl panties, and I could give my presentation standing up. Hot ass and all. I know you're dying to know what happened. My input wasn't headed. Rebranding commenced nationally, but I did avoid the burn center, so that's a positive. And just because why not, I'll have you know that after the millions were spent on rebranding, just a few years later, those millions were spent again on going back to market-level naming conventions. Perhaps the girl with the hot ass was worth listening to, is all I'm saying.

I laughed out loud recently at a meme that said that people who drink coffee every morning are psychotic. You know what reality looks like, and yet you're like, YES, I want to be wide awake for this bullshit. I'm like, well, no, but alcohol before 7 am is frowned upon. So pick your vice, and may the odds be ever in your favor. Because people, it's the real-life hunger games out there.

I took my coffee addiction on a road show a few years ago. Or more of a social media celebration show. For many months, I posted some sort of coffee meme daily. Some were catchy. Some were sad. Some were hysterical. Some held secret meanings, but only a few were caught. But all were so well received that folks still send them to me or tag me in coffee related posts years later. #procaffeinator took on a life of its own. It reaffirmed that many of life's little things are truly the source of joy. Finding joy in my morning coffee and sharing that joy with others. Little things make the world go round. Even the sad bean juice some folks choose to drink plain. Me? Plain? I think not. Mine always has just a splash of cream and a little bit of sweetener. And sometimes, I add a little treat in the evenings with some Baileys or Kahlua. If I'm really indulging, it's a Carajillo for me! Shaken, not stirred, please. Sitting on the deck of our little cabin in the woods with my mug of coffee is pure joy to me. Add hard rain coming down on the tin roof, and man, oh man....I'm in heaven! Early rainy mornings with a good cup of coffee snug under a blanket. Just the thought of it makes me feel warm and fuzzy inside.

It's been several years since I posted consistently on the topic, but to this day, folks send me coffee memes they find online. I recently got a sweet message on Facebook Messenger from someone who had taken a trip to Prague. She sent me a picture of the beautiful coffee mug she brought home. I told her it was gorgeous and looked like it would fit her hand and warm her soul for years to come. Yes, I "try on" my coffee mugs. And my purses, but that's a different topic altogether. They have to fit just right. The perfect mug fits just right in your hand. Right up against the palm without a gap. I figure no thigh gap, no palm gap!

There are days when my energy level is that of a sloth on Xanax. That yawn that keeps creeping in is actually a silent scream for coffee! On these days, oh who am I kidding, on ALL days I am the little engine that could… but coffee first! Because without it this hot mess express is at risk of becoming a full-blown shit show! I think all of us can identify with this one, especially single, working mothers. I don't know how I'd cope if it weren't for coffee. Seriously. If drinks could talk: Coffee - You can do this! Wine -You don't have to do this! Tequila - Holy shit! Did you really just do that?

I've always wanted to visit Africa, and now I know why. It's the birthplace of coffee! It dates back centuries when Ethiopians were thought to have harvested coffee beans from the great coffee forests of the Ethiopian plateau. I don't know much about Ethiopia. I've been told it's a beautiful country. But I do know I'd visit it just to find the birthplace of coffee so I can pay my respects to the geniuses who brought us this elixir of wakefulness. My dream vacation is to enjoy coffee in its birthplace and a gorilla safari, but I digress.

Even though I might be a caffeine addict, I like to consider myself a conscious addict. Meaning that I am aware of gimmicks like the world's most expensive coffee, which, according to the Specialty Coffee Association of America, just tastes bad. If you've never heard of Kopi Luwak, it's an "exclusive" and very expensive brand of coffee that's made from poop. Well, not entirely. It's made from coffee beans eaten by civets (a mongoose-like animal) in Indonesia that are partially digested and then defecated, just to be picked out and cleaned, roasted, and sold for a pretty penny worldwide. It's the novelty of it that makes it so popular. It's by no means good coffee.

Poop-coffee aside, I love it when my coffee kicks in, and I realize what an adorable, non-homicidal badass I'm going to be today.

Chapter 20

Self-Care & a Safe Space

I feel like we've come a long way as a society as a whole in becoming more aware of how the stresses and obstacles of everyday life can lead to a myriad of illnesses. More than becoming aware, we've finally become a tiny bit more tolerant of needing help. But we still have a very long way to go.

It took me a long time (too long) to realize that I want to build a life for myself and my son that doesn't only allow for living and having fun on weekends and holidays. A life we don't need a vacation from to feel sane again. I don't feel like a life where the first five days after the weekend are the hardest is something to aspire to. Whoever came up with the 5-day workweek idea - I hope your crotch gets infested by fleas and that your arms are too short to reach for you to scratch. That dude seriously screwed us over. Of course, it had to be a man who came up with such an idea. (It was Henry Ford who came up with it. Luckily, I don't drive a Ford) Five days a week was great for men! Out of the house earning a living meant they could escape the household duties and feel good about it! Unfortunately for women, once we joined the workforce, it meant we were out of the house those same five days but then still had to execute all the other household and family related responsibilities bestowed upon us. 'Super Mom' remember? And don't even think about having any time left for us. Don't get me wrong, I'm very grateful to those who fought for all these rights, but man alive! Perhaps the five days a week was what was needed at a certain time in history, but times have changed. In this technological era, we are 24/7/365 as it is. Kinda like daylight savings!? For the love of God, can someone please get rid of that too? Such a huge portion of people work remotely and from home these days. The Great Resignation during COVID-19 is proof of people's discontent with the current state of affairs. It just doesn't work anymore.

Self-care has become a buzzword on social media lately. However, I don't always feel like people truly understand what it means to practice self-care. I think for most, the word brings up pictures of luxurious spa days and massages. Those are great, but it's not necessarily what's meant with self-care. We've all heard the saying, *"You can't pour from an empty cup,"* which is absolutely true. But have you ever stopped to consider that self-care might mean doing what you usually avoid doing but need to do for your well-being? Things like saying NO when you need rest instead of allowing your people-pleasing tendencies to get the better of you. Not feeling guilty for NOT getting sucked into that pile of unfolded laundry that's become a tiny mountain in its own right the ONE evening you have a chance to just sit and catch your breath! Setting goals for your physical health, like eating healthy and working out, even when you don't feel like it. Self-care is taking time out to pamper yourself, but more importantly, doing what you need to do in order to take care of your overall well-being.

This last fall, I was booked to go with Dad to Houston for his radiation planning scan after they found some new lymph node involvement. We were set to leave in a couple of days when I got sick. I mean my 12-year-old tending to me, not going to work or even taking work calls, lost my voice, couldn't get out of bed, kinda sick. Finally, I called and went to see my doctor, telling him I was sure it was viral because I had no fever, etc. He tested me for everything and said, *"Well, the good news is you're still a badass nurse because your assessment is right on. Bad news is it's viral, and you're going to have to let it run its course."* I'm not a pansy when it comes to illness, but this kicked my ass for a week, and it took nearly six weeks to fully recover. Negative for flu, COVID, RSV, and strep, but I felt and looked like death. I truly believe in my heart of hearts that this was the universe telling me that since I wasn't resting and taking care of myself, it was doing it for me. Honestly, I think it was more like the universe screaming at the top of its lungs 'sit your ass down woman, or else'!

I had been running absolutely non-stop for over a year since Dad's diagnosis doing what I do. Powering through. Telling myself to *"Suck it up, buttercup, and get it done."* There will be time to rest when I'm dead. My job. My kid. My dad. My family. My job. My kid. My dad. My family. My job. My kid. My dad. My family. I'd forgotten me. I'd forgotten that if I died, who would do all the things for all the people? Now, was I on my deathbed? No. Let's not be dramatic. It's not as though I had a Man-cold. I just had a bad virus. But I do think this was the universe or my body turning on the tsunami warning system and waking my ass up. Take care of me before I ended up not being here to take care of anyone at all.

This was a huge wake-up call for me. Pivotal really. It made me think about my priorities and realize that me, myself, and I had to be in that top tier, or I was in big trouble. That right now, AJ and I were my #1 responsibility. That I wanted to be there and do everything I could for Dad, but I couldn't do it all by myself.

I think of this when I ask myself, "Where was your latest flight to Allie?" The handle. My latest flight was off the fucking handle! There are weeks when I think that if I don't survive this one, I'll take my straight jacket in hot pink, and I want my helmet to sparkle. Just don't deny me my coffee, even if I have to sip it through a straw.

My sanctuary is my home. During the last year of my marriage, I dreaded being home. My home had lost its peace and after finding a hidden camera with a listening device attached, I was no longer comfortable in my own house. It transported me back to my childhood memories of having to walk on eggshells around everyone. Constantly trying not to offend, upset, or trigger my brother because the wrath would follow. The *"Why did you say that"* or *"Why did you do that?"* *"You knew it would cause a reaction."* Being the peacekeeper is exhausting, and growing up, I'd just lock myself in my room and spend a lot of time alone to avoid it all. I think this is why, to this day, I NEED my alone time to recharge and settle. I enjoy my peaceful mornings with my cup of coffee and my journal, a good book, or sometimes just sitting silently and taking it all in. Unfortunately, when the eggshell walking is in your own home as an adult or in your marriage, you can't just lock yourself in your room to avoid conflicts. I recall driving home from work on the Friday of a long holiday weekend, wondering how I'd make it through three full days at home. I vowed when my ex moved out on my 40th birthday that I would NEVER lose the peace of my sanctuary again. That can be challenging with ongoing family dynamics, but it's all about the types of boundaries you set with both yourself and those who play a role in your life.

One of my favorite self-care things to do is to light candles. There's just something about them. The flicker of the flame that, when stared into and focused on, can help with meditation and vagus nerve calming. The scent can bring calm with a memory of something we hold dear. The feeling of being a bit extra or spoiling ourselves with a little treat. I've nearly always got a candle going, and it has become a soothing ritual for my mind.

I am finally at a point in my life where I will absolutely not deal with anything I don't fucking have to or want to. I'll leave, unfriend, unfollow, block, and do anything I need to do to deal with people and situations where I'm not respected or valued. I always thought if I communicated enough, there would be change. But that's not the case. You can communicate until you run out of breath, but your words are useless if there's no comprehension. My peace is my priority. BOUNDARIES people! It's a game-changer, I tell ya.

Sometimes, standing your ground and standing in your power might mean standing alone, and that's okay. I don't know about you, but I've allowed myself to be the people pleaser and peacekeeper to my own detriment for a long enough time. I've been the bigger, kinder, and more understanding person for longer than I should've allowed myself to be in many aspects of my life both personally and professionally. It took me until age 45 to realize that no one was coming. No one was coming to save me. No one was coming to stand up for me. No one was coming to fight my battles for me. No matter how hard I tried or what all I did, I would always be an outsider looking in. That was never going to change. What changed was a shift in my thoughts. If I'm an outsider looking in and am not welcomed with open arms, then why continue trying so desperately to seek approval and have the doors opened? Instead realizing if I wanted the attacking text tirades to stop, I had to stop them. If I wasn't going to tolerate certain behaviors from my son, I could not then sit idly by and allow them to be modeled to him by other grown ass adults. It has been incredibly painful and difficult at times, but through it all AJ and I are closer than ever, and I learned quickly that family isn't strictly about blood relations. It is about who is there for you in life and loves and supports you unconditionally. I no longer subscribe to the idea that blood is thicker than water and family sticks together. Blood makes relatives. Love and kindness and grace makes family. When I have a moment of doubt, all I need to do is to look at my son. He is happier, healthier, and doing better than he has in years. He gets into my car after school and when I say how was your day, he often says good, and sometimes he even says great! Sounds trivial, but it had been a few YEARS since that occurred. Stability, unconditional love, accountability, and peace have h made all the difference in the world.

Stand up for yourself! Use your voice even if it shakes! There is a quote that a dear friend sent me that reads "If you have to sacrifice your voice to 'keep the peace', it's no longer peaceful. You're internalizing the chaos instead" – Zara Bas

Just because you have developed the ability to understand why someone might behave in a certain way or why they are the way they are doesn't make it right and it sure as hell doesn't mean you have to continue to put up with it. That goes for co-workers, friends, and family members alike. It can be more painful when shitty behavior comes from the people we love and should be able to depend on, but it's far more harmful to tolerate it from them, as well as it has a far deeper impact. No amount of empathy or understanding should ever precede your own well-being. No matter who it comes from, if their behavior causes you pain or discomfort on a mental, emotional, or physical level, you need to either draw a line or walk away. And yes, it really is as simple as that. Simple does NOT mean easy. It means the DECISION to prioritize ourselves and the choice of our own wellbeing is easy, NOT that the action of doing so and some of the ramifications will be. We humans like to complicate things for ourselves, but nearly everything in life is a choice. You either choose to hold on to that which does not serve you, or you choose to invest your time and effort into protecting yourself and doing what is best for YOU!

You're not responsible for other people's thoughts, feelings, or behavior. Someone else's conduct does not reflect your character. Your character is independent of other people's appreciation. Your value is not found in other people's recognition of you. Your price tag is independent of what others think of you and how they may treat you. If you have shared your worth and demonstrated your value, and they still do not appreciate you, don't diminish your value by offering discounts. Don't force yourself to be less than what you are by continuing to show up consistently and working yourself to death to "prove your worth" to people who will never see or appreciate it. This can be a hard concept to accept, especially when discussing family and friends. At the end of the day, you have to practice your freedom of choice. What's more important? What others gain from your forgiving nature, or your sense of peace, your health, and your happiness?

You get to choose your value. You get to choose what you will and will not accept. You get to take care of yourself and continue to grow, with or without them. Stop betraying yourself for the comfort or even satisfaction of others. Picking yourself, validating your own feelings, and learning to walk away from what doesn't serve you, no matter how painful it may be, is perhaps the ultimate form of self-care. When it is family, it is that much more difficult. Society preaches that 'family is everything' and we must do everything 'for the good of the family'. But what if it comes at a tremendous personal cost? The thing that shook me into action was the fact that if what was happening and being perpetrated against me was done by anyone outside of the family circle, everyone would have been irate! However, because it was a family member, no one wanted to discuss, attempt to rectify, or even acknowledge it. I realized in that moment it was me or the family, and with great pain I picked me. I had to ensure I was here to raise my son. My why.

God, grant me the serenity to accept that this planet is filled with assholes and fuckery I cannot change, the courage to rise above said assholery and fuckery, and the wisdom to know that I'm worthy despite the opinions of assholes. Amen.

I'm curious. Do you also allow your heart to be broken to fulfill the needs of others? To ensure THEIR feelings aren't hurt at the cost of your own. That their needs are met as yours remain unfulfilled? Everyone wants a strong, powerful woman until they realize that she isn't going to tolerate their bullshit, she doesn't actually need them for survival, and they'll have to step up their own game to remain in your life.

Cher's mother once told her, "You know, sweetheart, one day you should settle down and marry a rich man." To which she replied, "Mom, I am a rich man." I love this. To me it validates my thought that I don't need a man to support me, to love me, or to even cheer me on. I'd love to have one that does all that and more, but I'm not going to die or even fail if that doesn't happen for me.

I mean let's be real. At this point, men aren't needed in the traditional sense. They aren't out hunting our dinner or fighting off wild animals or members of some other tribe. Hell, scientists have even created sperm cells from human bone marrow, so as futuristic as that may seem, I guess we no longer need them for reproduction technically. I'd always wanted a child and when I turned 30 and wasn't sure a man of marriage quality was in my future, my mom nearly fainted when I said if I didn't find that kind of love, I'd visit a sperm bank and do it myself. I must admit, my ex and I did at least breed well, so no regrets there. Vibrators and other erotic toys can do a far better job than many men can in the pleasure department, and did I mention that other than running out of batteries, there's no added stress as to whether or not they're functional. Most women are working and doing just as much to support the family financially as the men are. Women make up nearly 50% of the global workforce now, and if you happen to live in Canada, that number is closer to 60%. Go, Beavers, pun absolutely intended!

On that note, one of my favorite memories with my uncle married to Auntie Coffee as she's called by AJ, was the laughs at the table the night we all debated about which nation had the better national animal. Canada with its beaver or the US with our bald eagle. It could have been far worse had Benjamin Franklin gotten his way and the US had selected the turkey as our national animal? Then again based on the most recent debate and political happenings, perhaps it was simply foresight. But I digress…all I'm saying is choose the men you like because they're good for you and you want them in your life, not because you need them.

You know what's even better than a man? A fur baby! I am a huge proponent of animal rescues. Feeling lonely? Rescue a dog or a cat, not a needy boy, in a man's body. Not a friend or family member you rescue over and over again, like Groundhog Day, with zero reciprocation or gratitude even. So many amazing, beautiful animals need and deserve good homes. You may be tempted to think that rescuing one dog won't change the world, but I can assure you it will change the world for that one pup. And maybe, just maybe, yours too. I know my babies have only enriched my life. I don't know what I'd do without them. There's a reason why dog spelled backward is god. Whatever your beliefs, I firmly believe that dogs are angels sent without wings so that they aren't easily spotted.

Buddy, my rescued deer chihuahua (a chihuahua on stilts essentially), and Amadeus, my cat and first fur baby after I left home I lost during Covid. It's never a good time to lose your babies, but this happening during Covid really brought me to my knees. I was working insane hours, literally driving oxygen, ventilators, and other equipment between my facilities. My son was with my folks for eight weeks because with schools closed, I didn't think it was the safest approach for me to go to the hospital to work every day and then take AJ back and forth to my elderly parents house after being around me at night. I really missed him. I remember being on facetime on his ipad he put in his easter basket as he ran around with it collecting Easter Eggs that year. Not sure I've ever felt so much heartache and guilt for doing what I thought was right at the moment. It was hard on everyone for sure. I don't think I would've survived all that happened during that crazy time, along with my predicating divorce, if it hadn't been for Dolly, my brindle boxer who got dumped in the parking lot of the humane society with a broken hip. That angel sat next to me and literally licked the tears rolling down my face as I sat bawling my eyes out the first few times my son went visiting his dad during and after the divorce. I'd never been separated from my son for so long a period at a time, and it really tore my heart in pieces. People I needed chose to judge and gossip or disappear, but not Dolly. She just loved me through it. No condescension in her stare. No harsh words in her bark. That gorgeous girl showed me love in its pure and simple form.

After Amadeus and Buddy passed during Covid, we adopted a stray kitten from a barn litter on a friend's property. Marshmallow, a.k.a. "Marshy," was solid white when we got him, hence the name. AJ initially wanted to call him McCreamy. Um, no. Now try explaining why not to a 10-year-old boy at the time. Good luck with that. So Marshmallow it was! Within a few months, he was full-on Siamese with a dirty gray coat, dark gray socks, and white toes. And yes, blue, crossed eyes. Bless his little heart. He is absolutely precious and he shakes his head back and forth as you approach him, trying to track you as you move. We call him the dog cat because he runs out to greet you along with the dogs when you get home, and he's very sociable and loving.

Last, but not least, is Noble. AJ gave him his name, but let me assure you, this pup is anything but noble! He's a white albino pure-bred boxer who was part of a friend's neighbor's litter. Not straight from the North Pole, as AJ was initially told and believed until just recently. Although there have been times since his arrival when I'd have happily paid full-price postage to send him there with no 'return to sender' address! He was gifted to us as a Christmas "gift," or maybe a "curse," more than two years ago. We couldn't decide if he was stupid or an asshole, but since then, we've clarified that he's both. He's unbelievably destructive and full of anxious energy. When I say destructive, I don't just mean the normal puppy kind of thing where they chew a couple of shoes or something. I mean, you can't have a dog bed for him because he EATS it! Not tears it apart and leave pieces everywhere. I mean, he literally EATS it! Same thing for ANYTHING left where he can reach it. Socks are his favorite, but don't worry, if AJ neglects to leave a sock where it's accessible to Noble, he will happily settle for a remote, a blanket, the edge of my comforter hanging off the bed, shoes, robes, and drywall, for God's sake! Put him outside, you say? Better make sure he can't find a stick or a rock to chew on and be aware that he will make sure that you and every neighbor in a five-mile radius is aware that you somehow forgot him in the backyard. Ceasar Milan…where are you when a girl needs you? He also has terrible allergies and is always either licking or scratching, which leads to bleeding, even when on meds that are supposed to keep him from licking or scratching for whatever reason. He's jealous as all get out so God forbid you love on or give attention to Dolly or Marshy. He will run over and insert himself between you and whoever you are loving on. But he's family, and we love him so much. I feel a great sense of comfort when he is lying next to me on the couch (or trying to sit on me with all 85 pounds as though he's a lap dog instead of a small horse), Dolly lying next to me on her bed, and Marshmallow on the windowsill nearby.

These are my fur babies and my comfort and support when I'm really down or in a dark place.

Music is my other form of self-care. I grew up with it as my Dad's a professional musician. He ran the Jazz program and Trumpet studies at the university level, started a longstanding, sought-after brass quintet, and played principal trumpet in several major symphony orchestras. And, by the way, still kills it at age 83, with lung cancer, no less!

I was in band, concert/jazz/marching all the way through high school and part of the way into college. Music has the power to communicate for us when we struggle to find the words ourselves. To wrap us in comfort when needed. To motivate us to keep moving and to help us relax and rest when necessary. Music transcends all! It can empower you when you need to pull out your badass strut or give you a pick-me-up when you're feeling a little blue. Music is a universal language everyone understands, regardless of culture, background, race, nationality, sex, gender, or beliefs.

I remember having a particularly rough few days with some pretty heavy family drama, a really sick kid causing us to miss work and school for an entire week, and just a whole lot of pressure from all directions. I received a text from an old friend saying that her daughter had made a video for me and was dedicating a song she was sending me on WhatsApp. Mind you, her daughter was born just shy of a year ahead of my AJ. Her mama was the first person, except my friend, the sonographer, who knew I was pregnant with AJ. Even before my husband at the time knew, she's that close a friend to me. She's an incredible single mom in her own right, helping support her mother and her daughter, and she does it all with a smile. I opened the video, and Ciara did a killer rendition of Jax's Cinderella Snapped. Man, oh, man, was that just what the doctor ordered! How can those lyrics not pump you up? (If you've never heard it, search for it on YouTube and turn up the volume!

"Once upon a time, there was a princess.

Waiting for a boy to give back her shoe.

Suck it in, suck it in, be a wife in a blue dress.

The prettiest piece of property the land ever knew.

She waited and she waited for the guy to show.

But she didn't know that after midnight.

He was busy in her stepsister's bed, So Cinderelly said: "Plot twist."

I don't need no prince to save me I'm a goddamn CEO.

Don't call me "Baby", equal pay me.

Snow White said you tried to kiss her, So I'll just buy a new glass slipper.

Burn your castle down.

And kids, that's how Cinderella snapped.

When the smoke cleared, every girl in the whole land Woke the fuck up and started making demands.

Rapunzel shaved their head so there was nothin' to climb on Jasmine made out with Mulan.

Sleeping Beauty sued the dude who kissed her while she was asleep, and Ariel was confident without any feet.

Tiana went and got a Biomedical Degree, and Beauty realized that she was the Beast.

He said, "Cindy, sweetie, don't be so emotional You're always so emotional It's fine to be controllable."

If I'm emotional, that'd be the reason for you to address me.

While you're on your knees in the scary event.

That I get too emotional during your trial, so watch how you're speaking.

Cause while you were sleeping around every weekend.

And using your power to pray on the weakest, I studied your own legislation all season.

And last I checked, cheating is treason!" [3]

When I feel frustrated over how other people are behaving or treating me, Kesha's "Bastards" song is my go-to. Crank it up and sing it with me!

"I got too many people, ba-da-da-da.

Got left to prove wrong.

All those motherfuckers, ba-da-da-da.

Been too mean for too long.

And I'm so sick of crying.

Darling, what's it for?

I could fight forever, oh-oh.

But life's too short.

Don't let the bastards get you down, oh no.

Don't let the assholes wear you out.

Don't let the mean girls take the crown. Don't let the scumbags screw you 'round. Don't let the bastards take you down.

Been underestimated my entire life I know people gonna talk shit, ba-da-da-da.

My entire life, know people gonna talk shit, ba-da-da-da.

And darling, that's fine.

But they won't break my spirit.

I won't let 'em win.

I'll just keep on living, keep on living though, the way I wanna live.

Don't let the bastards get you down, oh no.

Don't let the assholes wear you out.

Don't let the mean girls take the crown. Don't let the scumbags screw you 'round.

Don't let the bastards get you down." [4]

When I'm having a moment with the asshole in my brain telling me I'm not enough, not worthy, or I can't possibly be successful? I crank up PINK's "Fuckin' Perfect."

"Made a wrong turn once or twice.

Dug my way out blood and fire.

Bad decisions, that's alright.

Welcome to my silly life.

Mistreated, misplaced, misunderstood.

Miss 'No way, it's all good.'

It didn't slow me down.

Mistaken, always second-guessing.

Underestimated.

Look, I'm still around.

Pretty pretty, please.

Don't you ever ever feel.

Like you're less than fucking perfect.

Pretty pretty, please.

If you ever ever feel.

Like you're nothing.

You're fucking perfect to me.

You're so mean when you talk about yourself. You were wrong.

Change the voices in your head.

Make them like you instead.

So complicated.

Look how we all make it.

Filled with so much hatred.

Such a tired game.

It's enough, I've done all I can think of chased down all my demons.

I've seen you do the same.

Oh, pretty pretty please.

Don't you ever ever feel.

Like you're less than fucking perfect." [5]

So many people are in therapy to learn how to deal with people who aren't. I'm many people. I'm the one who's in therapy because some people in my life refuse to go for therapy. I have family who will do therapy but refuse to try medication and others who will do medication but refuse to go for therapy. Imagine if they could just cross-pollinate. That would be perfect. I know that there are people in the world who love to pill-shame those who need it. Fuck off is what I have to say to them.

When you need help, you utilize every tool that's available to you. There's nothing courageous about shaming others for doing what they need to do for their health when you haven't spent even a minute in their shoes.

Sometimes, courage looks like quietly walking away and allowing others their opinions without fighting back. No throwing of punches. No yelling back. No trying to prove you're right. No getting in the last word. Rather, choose to maintain your dignity and wisdom over immaturity. Practicing self-control and regulating your own emotions. Self-control is the rarest and boldest of flexes in today's world.

Here are some things I've said to my therapist,

- "I know that everything happens for a reason, but WHAT. THE. ACTUAL. FUCK?"

- "I've got everybody else, but who's got me?"

- "Is wine allowed here?"

- "So I was young and dumb once, then I tried optimism and being hopeful, now I'm at fuck it all. Is there a pill for that, or is this normal?"

- "Does listening to all of this make you therapissed?"

Therapy is awesome. Really, it is. I suggest everyone should go to therapy regularly. The world would be such a better place for it. But then we have those who think they know it all and don't need therapy (denial) and those who believe that therapy is just a money-making scheme (ignorance). In my opinion, people who are against therapy are those who are scared of facing their problems and their role in creating those problems. Or those who just do not want to face what they've been through because it's too scary. I mean, they don't say, "Welcome to shrink in the box. May I take your disorder?" So, you need to be ready to do the work. And it is hard work, and it can be scary for sure. But oh, is it worth it! I keep trying to get my therapist to come to a family holiday or at least shadow me for a day, but so far, no luck. I really think there would be some wow factor to that, but whatevs.

Routine and self-care, baby. Those are superpowers you need to invest in. Look after your hygiene. Brush your teeth twice a day. Keep your house neat. Eat healthy foods. Move your body regularly. Get your hair done and maintain it. I read a sign once in a beauty salon years ago: "I'm a beautician, not a magician." I call bullshit. That fresh cut and styled feeling is MAGIC! Ask any woman. Same goes for fingernails. When I'm incredibly stressed or upset, I pick at them and end up with man hands and no artificial nails…insert sad face. Having a mani/pedi periodically as part of your routine and self-care is something I enjoy and always makes me feel better. I love my time at Mimi's nails!!

Other people are not medicine! It took me years to figure that out. You need to learn how to love and take care of yourself. It's hard to do, but it's a must. There's no chance of a healthy relationship if you do not know and love yourself truly first. You cannot give what you do not have.

Then there's the CTRL + ALT + DELETE tool that should be used on a regular basis.

- **Control yourself** - learn how to control which thought you allow yourself to focus on, how to regulate your emotions, and how to choose your behavior on a daily basis.

- **Alter your thinking** - take the time to invest in learning what negative thinking patterns you may be a victim of without knowing it. Participate in an online course that teaches CBT (Cognitive Behavioral Therapy), which will teach you all about cognitive distortions and automatic negative thoughts.

- **Delete negativity** - this applies to negative people (those energy vampires), negative feeds on social media, negative vibes, and any negativity that makes you feel drained of your energy.

And realize that on the days that you only have 40% to give and you give 40%, you've given 100%.

Wear socks with positive, pick-me-up messages that only you can see. Some of my favorites are mine that say "MotherFuckingGirlPower." My "but 1st coffee" socks are a close second. And then, for the really rough days, there's the "fuck off" socks.

Something else I also only discovered later in life is waxing. Who knew that having your nether region waxed could feel so incredibly empowering? Sounds a little masochistic, doesn't it? I thought so, too, until I tried it, and I am never going back. If you haven't seen the waxing scene in the movie Bad Moms, go watch it. You're welcome. But seriously there is just something about it. I mean laying there spread eagle with your most private areas totally exposed and entrusted to an esthetician? The vulnerability! We gut laugh and talk about all sorts of things, all the while I'm there with my bare butt in the air or flat on my back legs spread. Jade is the bomb and I'll never go to anyone else. I've told her she can retire or whatever, but I'll just come to the house for services. Hiding that appointment on your work calendar can be fun. I used to just put PP, but then I was asked and thought, "How the hell do I explain 'pussy prep'?" All joking aside, though, if you haven't, try it. It's a game-changer.

I look at all these young and energetic people with their fancy social plans, and I'm like, "*Have fun at your party, people; I'm gonna be President Pajamas of Netflix Nation.*" I don't quite know exactly what age it happens, but at some point, trying to have a conversation while screaming into someone else's ear over loud music just isn't fun anymore. Looking after yourself becomes way more fun. Early nights, cozy pajamas, peace and quiet. That's what I'm talking about.

It's so important to learn to take time out for yourself. Even if you are encumbered with spawnlings, we all need time to ourselves on a regular basis. It's important. It's what allows us to check within and do whatever we need to look after ourselves. Whether it's going on a hike to get some fresh air and a bit of exercise, sitting with earphones listening to your favorite music while coloring, reading, napping, going for a massage, having lunch with your friends, seeing the counselor, etc., whatever it is, you must look after yourself. Again, you cannot pour from an empty cup. The more you look after yourself, the more capacity you have to give to others. We so often fall into this trap of enmeshment where we almost melt into the person we're in a relationship with. It's unhealthy and unsustainable. You're an individual with individual needs, and so are they. Learn to take care of yourselves individually; the surplus is for one another and whoever else needs it. You can and should only pour from your cup when it is full. What you share with others should be what you have in excess, not what barely sustains you.

Also, learn when it's time to let go. There isn't always a solution. Sometimes, you just need to accept something for what it is, chuck it in the fuck-it bin, and move on. There's no use in hanging on to something if it hurts you or is useless to you. Toss it like Roger Staubach did a pig skin.

While you're at it, put that same amount of vigor into your choice of attitude. Pessimists see their glass as always being half empty. Optimists see theirs as half full. Realists have already cracked open the next bottle to pour another glass. You need to be able to see things for what they are. Not everything is a crisis. You don't have to reply to every asshole keyboard warrior sitting on the other side of the globe in their underwear who's trolling your comments section. A nasty "gram" (rude email) from your boss without any requested information to be delivered, delete. A nasty comment on a social media post, delete. A text thread attacking your personal character…DELETE! A vaguely worded card after an extensive absence that neither takes responsibility nor apologizes for what led to the separation in the first place doesn't deserve the mental spiral and panic of what to say back. You don't have to give every energy-sucking vampire who comes your way your attention. Having your heart broken is not the end of the world. Yes, it sucks, but it's also an opportunity from which to learn and grow.

There's so much beauty and opportunity in the world for those who care to take the time to see it. If you want to be happy, start focusing your attention on the beauty that surrounds you on a daily basis. The first blooming flowers of Spring. A butterfly that crosses your path. The stars at night. When was the last time that you just sat and watched the stars at night? Stopped and smelled the roses? Enjoyed the laugh of your child?

There's that saying that goes, "Change your attitude, and you change your altitude." It's true. Everything is about your mindset and how you choose to see the world. The meaning you choose to assign to life's events. What you choose to focus on on a daily basis. Who you choose to allow to have access to you. How you choose to allow people to treat you.

It's all a choice, my friend. Yes, we may not choose what happens to us every day, but we do get to choose how to react to it. Your trauma and pain might not be your fault, but your healing is 100% your responsibility.

Focusing on the negative and allowing yourself to adopt a negative mindset makes an already difficult journey so much more difficult. Unnecessarily so. You may be handed a cactus here and there, but no one said you have to shove it up your ass! I know the shift can be challenging and there are times it feels impossible, but baby steps.

Hakuna-Mavodka…what a wonderful phrase. Hakuna-Mavodka…it means no memories for the rest of your night. **Come on! Sing it with me!**

Chapter 21

Women Tribe

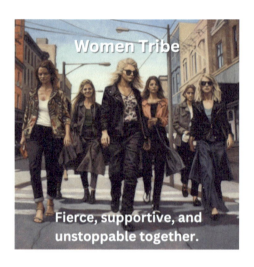

You know what I love? I love it when strong women stick up for one another and when women choose to lift one another up instead of breaking each other down like catty wenches. We have enough struggles as a sex as it is, so why pile on?

I don't know where I'd be without my women tribe. These are my core people. They're the ones who can call you out on your shit, knowing that you know it's out of love. The ones who can say, "*Hey girl, your crazy is showing. You might want to tuck that shit back in*!" These are the type of friends who'll have your back in any room, even when you're not there. These women are priceless, but sadly, they're few and far between in this modern world. Nowadays, it's all about superficial competition and keeping up with the Kardashians. Let me just tell you, those picture-perfect photos you see them flaunting on Instagram? It's not based on reality. No thanks! I'll stick to my mom's squad of real-life working mom heroes trying to raise good humans. Kick-ass women who don't judge when shit gets messy and dive in to help without being asked. The badass broads who say, "*Same, Sis*," and mean it when you think you surely must be cracking. The boss babe who not only works full-time in a high-pressure job while raising a young girl, killing it as a wife, and getting her Ph.D. but also gives you the new word "Twatwaffle" to help you describe a woman you are struggling with who is just that. The woman who may not have the degrees and the certifications but has the brains, the intestinal fortitude, and the knowledge to blow your ass out of the water! My attorney friend that had a stroke with her 1st child and had to literally learn to walk again but is thriving with her now TWO daughters and a career! Now, those are my people!!

Life is way too short to hang out with anyone other than those who raise you up. There are enough people who want to tear you down just because they can. Not even because of anything you did. Just because they feel like it or think it somehow gives them a leg up, screw them. You just need to focus on what is within your control, and that is who and what you give your time and energy to. Both of these are finite, so choose wisely!

Here's a little example from an experience that taught me the importance of a women's tribe.

I was with a big healthcare company since I received a scholarship from them in nursing school. I thought I'd work there forever, but leadership changed, culture changed, and I found myself asked to do something that would break my #1 rule about doing what's right even if it costs you dearly. My rule says, "Whatever decisions I make must be with the desire to always be proud of who I am and what I stand for and to always be able to look myself in the mirror." So, I left when an opportunity plopped in my lap at the exact moment I realized I had to leave this place.

Unbeknownst to me, I would be pregnant in a couple of months, unprotected by FMLA, along with no PTO (personal time off) accumulated, and the need to continue to pay health insurance while out delivering my baby. I'm not a hair-on-fire person, but I was kinda freaking out. My job could be filled. I had no income to support my family. Yikes!

In comes a woman, still a dear friend to this day, who donated a few weeks of her own PTO to me. To me! Unasked. Unexpectedly. Just because she could. When I got the call from HR to tell me, I was brought to my knees in relief and gratitude. I took the three weeks off after my c-section to bond with my new baby and was paid my normal rate, insurance covered, and all because this person took it upon themselves to help me when I needed it and lift me up so I could do what I needed to. THAT'S a forever friend and the best type of person to have in your tribe.

Or how about my #lifers? This is a couple who came to my aid when I desperately needed them. I'd had a VERY invasive surgery and was staying in a hotel in their city recovering because that specialty, in particular, isn't available where I live, and I wasn't released to travel home for a bit. I knew one of them pretty well after having worked together and bonded for a few years, but that first night I needed help getting back into my abdominal binder after my shower, she was working. So here comes the knock at the hotel room door declaring special delivery, and it's her wife. Now keep in mind I'd met her wife a total of ONE TIME! Yes, we're all nurses, but still. Here is this amazing woman I've met all of once on her hands and knees, checking my incisions and my drain with her face at crotch level and my ass standing there in all my naked glory. Completely mortified but with no choice. I needed help. I couldn't bend to see the entire incision, and I couldn't fasten that abdominal binder to hold all my shit in place on my own. So here we were. We both nearly passed out laughing when I asked if she was enjoying the view. I told her I could never thank her enough, and you know what she said to me? She said, "You already have. You helped my wife to see how incredibly talented she truly is. You lifted her up, supported her, and gave her joy. I'm just paying you back." Wow! Now you understand the #lifers.

A friend recently sent me a meme that hilariously hit home. It read something like, "I'm really the multipurpose friend. I'm down for brunch, church, aggravated assault, working out, whatever... just let me know." Or how about the one that says, "If standing up for yourself burns a bridge, I have matches, and we ride at dawn!" No matter the circumstances, I've got your back. Fierce friendships amongst women can best be explained by the Dixie Chicks song Goodbye Earl. This type of ride-or-die friendship is all I have room for in my life nowadays. I'd been part of a small group of women and we had a group text thread going for several years. My BFF with whom I'd fallen out was part of that thread as well. I'd continued to interact and join in but each time I saw her name pop up it came with a stomach pain or a heart pang. I finally left the conversation for good and text the other members that I'd love to continue our friendship but the constant reminder of what once was and the fakeness of pretending all was well wasn't good for me. Life is short, and I don't have the fake in me. Never have and never will. I refuse. To be more realistic, I'm less of a Goodbye Earl and more of a Lady Gaga's Grigio Girls kinda supporter, but fierce, nonetheless. And if you're not, take care. Some of the saddest and most painful goodbyes are to those who were once your fiercest supporters and you theirs.

Kindness costs nothing. Decency costs nothing. Neither does giving what you have more than enough of to someone else in need. You'll never run out of what is meant for you.

On the flip side of this coin, you have women who can be insecure and feel threatened. Or women who have made it and see no value in responding to or supporting others to do the same. Those you reach out to because you have a business proposition that you feel could really positively impact them, but they don't have the time of day to respond to an email or a text for a chat. These women are unfortunately more common, and boy, can they hurt. I luckily have enough life experience and hours spent in therapy to know that the way they are has nothing to do with me. People project their fears and insecurities in peculiar ways sometimes. And some just rise to a level where they forget that their shit stinks just as badly as anyone else's. If you pay close enough attention, you'll notice all the unresolved pain people walk around with and how it causes them to behave.

You will always be too much for some people. Those are simply not your people, and that's more than okay. The last thing you want is to be stuck between an energy vampire and a stab-you-in-the-back-first-opportunity-that-comes-around kind of person. You won't be everyone's cup of tea. Do you know why? Because you're champagne, darling!

I keep my circle very small. They say the faker you are, the bigger your circle, and the more real you are, the smaller your circle. I'm very real. If you're lucky enough to be a part of my circle, don't lose your spot by being a shady ass motherfucker. If you do choose that path though, I will go quietly. I will not challenge the lies you tell yourself and others regarding what occurred. You and I both know that what I shared with you I did from the heart. Not out of jealousy as you propose, but out of genuine heartfelt concern for you regarding the man in your life. Your picker is broken, and I've witnessed you choose too many bad ones to not speak up. I feared you had dove headfirst into a REALLY detrimental situation with the potential of destroying many aspects of your life. You were my person, and I could not have lived with myself if I didn't share my angst. I have no ill will and genuinely hope things don't go the way my fear feels they will, but I will not be there to know this time. I've gotten better about truly screening who is sitting at my table and removing them if they prove unworthy of the level of access and care I put into my friendships. It's not that I don't want you to eat, just not at my table.

My Mimi. My mom's mom once told me that if we are incredibly lucky, we can fill one hand when counting our dearest friends when we leave this earth. The older I get, the more I realize she was spot on. Some that once held a place on that hand change and lose their place there. Others move on just because of life circumstances but maintain their position because of all we did, learned, and experienced together. The best stay until one of you moves on from this plane of existence and hopefully meet you on the other side…roasting marshmallows perhaps?

I only want and need people in my life who will be there for me when the shit gets real. Friendships and their fortitude are tested in the difficult times we have to navigate, not when all is going well and we're flying high. Real friends are those who come and sit in the shit with you when things seem to be falling apart. When you're navigating a divorce and being judged by all. When there's an unexpected diagnosis or illness. When there's a death of a family member, and you're struggling. When you're going through a depressive episode and can't even get out of bed. When you pick your own mental health and heart along with that of your son's and lose family. Those are true friends. The kind of people who will listen to what it is you need, even if it means simply just listening to me rant on instead of trying to "fix" it when I just need to rant on—someone who not just hears me but actually *listens*. Sometimes I just need someone to simply be there… not to fix anything or do anything in particular, but to just allow me to feel like I'm supported and cared about and reminded that I'm not totally batshit crazy! That my feelings are valid and what I remember happening, really did happen.

I have a multitude of superficial relationships with folks in my outer circle. Not friendships as much as acquaintances. We exchange societal pleasantries of how are you? How are the kids? How's work? It doesn't mean I don't care or I have any ill will towards them. It's just that I'm not invested in their lives, nor are they in mine. One of the hardest things I've experienced is when an inner circle person becomes more of a superficial acquaintance when a change in your friendship is so significant that the entire relationship shifts. When you provide feedback or well-intended warnings about a choice they are making, and *poof*, just like that, they disappear into the background. It's hard. Gut-wrenching even. But in the end, if a friendship can so easily devolve so substantially and with such finality, was it ever the friendship you thought it was? I'm undecided here, but I do know that those in my inner circle are very few in number, but they're there. Unwavering in their love and support of me and of my decision to start picking myself, my mental health, and my heart above all else.

A close friend of mine, a badass nurse leader in her own right, and I found ways to support each other during Covid. Everyone else was quarantined at home, and we were in the fight of our lives, leading during an unprecedented pandemic. We were desperately understaffed with nowhere near enough resources or equipment. Surrounded by death, of not only patients, but of colleagues, friends, and family as well. Trying to be strong and support our teams while doing everything we could not to just collapse and fall ourselves. Dark humor and ridiculous meme exchanges were our go-to communication to sustain each other. We didn't have time to talk or catch up while we were trying to play our part in saving the world(or at least our little piece). But shooting a meme over that would likely make other people blush or question your sanity was a lifeline to us. Dark humor is born from trauma. It's how many of us cope. If you ever come across someone with a dark yet hilarious sense of humor, know there's trauma somewhere in their past. I can almost guarantee it.

Or they work in healthcare. Who else can eat food stored for freshness in Ziplock biohazard bags while giving a detailed report about body fluids and wound drainage? Another dear friend of mine I've had since college is someone I can't imagine navigating life without. She knows it all. The good, the bad, and the ugly. I know that she's always in my corner. She and her husband hosted me for a bottle of Dom Perignon and a celebratory brunch when I received a promotion. She's a straight shooter, and we're always brutally honest with each other. Our friendship has survived over the decades and will always remain strong because of just that. It's the judgment-free zone. The sarcasm runs high, and the dark humor is unparalleled, which is spectacular, but the loyalty and unconditional love here is the true gift. It's usually the ones who have faced the most heartache in this world that do their utmost to make others laugh. I think it's because they know what it's like to feel like you may never laugh again and don't want anyone else to feel that way. It's a dark place, and the pandemic surely brought a lot of us close to entering that place. Some are perhaps still trying to get out of it. This is when we all need a friend who can come and fetch us, wherever we are, and walk us back to the light. The two of us have enough inside jokes to fill an ocean and have navigated some of life's most difficult challenges together, and I feel sure we always will!

I recently took a trip of a lifetime with a boss-bitch friend of mine. She's a wonderful therapist who started her business several years ago and is doing incredibly well. No, Karen, unfortunately for me, not the kind of therapist I need a free lifetime membership of services with, but rather a physical/occupational type therapist that specializes in pediatrics. It was totally unplanned, a spur-of-the-moment thing. It went something like this: I got a text inviting me to happy hour the Friday before Thanksgiving.

I declined because I'd had AJ, and we were supposed to be celebrating his 12th birthday. I offered to catch up in the week of Thanksgiving as an alternative since AJ would be with his dad. Since I'd drawn a hard boundary of no longer traveling with my brother, I would not be headed to Colorado with the family. She replied, saying that she couldn't because she was heading out of town for a long weekend for her cousin's wedding. I jokingly said, "Nice! Where are we going?" To which she replied, "Cartagena, Colombia." I was still joking and asked if I'd fit in her suitcase. I laughed it off until she said, "You should come with me!" I debated for about 30 seconds, threw caution to the wind, and booked a flight right then and there. This is SO not me. Last minute plans to leave the country and travel somewhere so foreign?! Well, I guess maybe it is me, because I did it! And I'd done it once before to visit a dear friend when my divorce finalized. She and her family were stationed in Germany and headed on a summer adventure. Shit, now that I think about it, I was a family road trip crasher joining their European vacation that fourth of July, and I guess I was a wedding crasher on the Colombia excursion. I guess the lesson here is really for everyone else in my life; don't invite me if you don't really want me to come because I'm likely to say yes!!!

I was 45 years old before my first business-class flight. And just like that, 96 hours later, we were on our way. Champagne, inflight movies and dinner, and warm moist hand towels? Yes please!! Four flights, three countries (I can also now say I've been to Ecuador and Panama in addition to Colombia), too many drinks, and nowhere near enough coffee later, an amazing time was had by all. We laughed until our bellies hurt and talked for hours on end about life and all that comes with divorce, single motherhood, aging parents, massive professional responsibilities, and so much more.

My favorite topic started when she asked me if I ever sometimes felt like I just didn't fit in. Ummm yeah! Have you met me? Currently, I'm the one white person (actually, there was one other white person, the mother of the groom) with two Mexicans, two half-breeds (I can say that as my son is half white and half Mexican), and about 150 Colombians. We laughed at the situation, but it started quite the conversation regarding being an educated, powerful businesswoman. How hard it is to find our people. How difficult it is to date. It's so nice to share moments like this and realize it's not just you! I ate and drank and laughed and SLEPT! I mean like 8 to 10 hours for two nights in a row uninterrupted, and woke rested for the first time in years, literally. I danced on a yacht! I even spent extra time plucking those blonde menopausal chin hairs, so I wasn't unintentionally waving at folks while on board. I attended and helped run point at quite possibly the most elaborate wedding I've ever attended and in the oldest church in Cartagena, to boot! I walked in the post-nuptial parade with the beating drums and ballerinas, as they're called, all decked out in their costumes. (Mimi, the groom's mother, who is a badass in her own right, made me laugh out loud when she said she was only still walking along because the humidity had made everything so slick, she was just sliding down the street at that point! You and me both, sister! ¡Calor está bien, húmido no me gusta!).

Side note: Mimi played single mom to her three kids after her husband (their father) decided she wasn't the woman for him. She put herself through school in her late thirties and became a fucking engineer who works on F-16s! What the what!? Mimi is a baddy in the very best way possible! She could've sulked and laid in bed and thought about all the things she SHOULD be doing to be able to provide for her family. She could've become a bitter and angry person full of resentment for the way her life had gone awry. Mimi could've thought and felt her way into a massive depression with all the things her ex SHOULD have done differently or all the things that she SHOULD do now. We ALL have to be careful when life throws us these curve balls because the immediate inclination is to crawl into bed, pull the covers over your head, and hope it all gets better. Sadly, we can "should" all over ourselves. We can "should" all over everyone around us. In the end we either "should ourselves" to death or we get up and act! Propel ourselves out of that very inviting pity party however we can to find our path forward and continue the journey!

I sat with all my new Colombian friends at the reception, doing my best to communicate and understand. My friend's five family members in attendance, and the massive familia de la novia were all just wonderful. They treated me with such kindness and grace you'd have thought I'd known them for years. I had no idea how badly I needed this four-day whirlwind trip, but man alive, was it well-timed and so wonderful and strangely enough given I was in a foreign country, one of my favorite Thanksgivings of all time!

I think Jane Fonda said, "*Friendship between women is different than friendship between men. It's my women friends that keep starch in my spine, and without them, I don't know where I would be. We have to just hang together and help each other.*" So, thank you my precious friend, not just for the adventure of a lifetime, but for being part of my tribe!

When we're down, we learn who our true friends are. And sometimes, the people you want to be a part of your entire story are only meant to play a role for a chapter or two. It can be difficult to let go, but I've recently learned that you can never lose anything that was always meant for you. And, sometimes, people cross our paths to teach us a lesson. Be grateful for them as well, even if the lesson rips your heart out. It's often a blessing in disguise.

Then there are those we must forgive without receiving a deserved apology because our forgiveness shouldn't be tied to their words but to our need to simply let go and move on for our own sanity and happiness.

I hope you'll choose to be that girl who roots for the other girl, tells a stranger that her hair looks amazing, and encourages other women to believe in themselves and their dreams. Choose to be *that* girl. The world needs more of *that* girl.

Realize that you are enough. You don't need anyone to complete you. You are a whole, perfectly imperfect person already. Losing love is okay. Losing your best friend is horrible, but okay. Losing family members, either to eternity or by choice, is completely heartbreaking and yet survivable. Losing yourself in the process of trying to get them back to you or to keep them in your life at enormous personal expense is not okay. Value yourself first! You are important, and you and your happiness always come first. Remember, you cannot give what you do not have!

Brene Brown is one of my favorite authors, speakers, and overall boss babes. She spoke of a conversation she had with her daughter as a young child regarding friends and what we look for in friends. She described a flame held in the palm of your hand for protection so it doesn't go out and the fact that the friends worth seeking out and having will cup your hands to further protect your flame. Encouragers, if you will. The ones we do NOT want to keep around are those who say nay. Those who don't encourage. Those who attempt to dull our flame or even blow it out. Flame blower outers are a hard no!

For example, when you're invited to contribute an article to a journal, and your "friend" says, "Oh, that's a stupid publication." Or you get a promotion at work, and they say, "Good luck with all the added work." These types aren't friends. They're friends in disguise, just waiting for you to trip and fall on your face so they can step over you and take your place.

You don't need these types of people in your life. Why not?

Because YOU ARE CHAMPAGNE, DARLING! And don't you forget it!

Chapter 22

AJ's Chapter

Everything in life revolves around the question, "*Why?*"

I love Simon Sinek's work. His groundbreaking TED talk on how great leaders inspire action, including his "start with why" theory, has made many people think about what drives them personally. What is your why?

Being a single parent can be hard AF. But my precious boy AJ is my why, and I wouldn't give up what we have for the world. I want AJ to see me successfully navigate every challenge I come across in life, even if I'm in a particular circumstance where success might be just to survive. I want him to see me learn from my struggles and teach him the difficult lessons I've learned, and I am still learning on a daily basis (sometimes far more often than I'd want). I want AJ to know that he's capable of achieving anything he chooses to go after but also to learn that life takes grit and sometimes just plain survival modes to do so. My son is my only child; he is my greatest achievement and biggest responsibility. My reason to continue to fight and work and push through those days where I'd really rather just "*latibulate*" (a 17th-century word I'm determined to bring back, which literally means to simply sit in the corner and hide from reality). I do what I do and keep putting one foot in front of the other because the alternative is to sit in the corner rocking back and forth while sucking my thumb. Somehow "*latibulate*" gives it more of an intellectual flare.

As my one and only child, I don't think he will ever truly understand the strength of my love for him. Not fully. He will forever be the only one on earth who knows what my heartbeat sounds like from the inside. Nothing in life will bring you to your knees faster than your baby, even when they're grown, as my mom friends with older children have so encouragingly shared.

Sometimes, I worry about and doubt myself and my approach as a mama. I think if they are being truthful, most if not all moms worry about their mothering and how it impacts our children. I had a conversation recently with a fellow mom whose children are grown, and she shared feeling partially at fault for a situation with one of her kids because she worries, she sheltered them too much. Her thought process was that because she'd sheltered them so much, they went wild in a way when they had their freedom. I chuckled and told her that sometimes I worry I'm doing the opposite. My approach has been to just be real about things because my thought has always been that I'd rather AJ learn about things from me than from others that may or may not be accurate sources. Sometimes the things AJ will say in front of me or discuss with me make me cringe, but I'd rather have some awkward moments now than him make bad decisions out of simple ignorance later. I'm not kidding myself into thinking I can prevent him from making poor choices here and there as we all do, but perhaps he'll at least think about it first. And even more importantly, feel comfortable calling me when he inevitably does screw up. I hate the idea of him ever being in a bad situation and NOT call me out of fear of how I will react. I want him to think "I need to call mama!", not "My mom is gonna kill me!".

There are no true hard-and-fast rules when it comes to parenting. There are the basics, like loving your child and caring for their basic needs, at the very least. But there's no one-size-fits-all handbook that tells you what to do in every single situation because everyone's different. I tell AJ that I'm learning as I go, just as he is, and that I will make mistakes. I tell him that I didn't get a copy of *How to Be a Mother for Idiots* when I gave birth. He'll ask how I know something or where I learned something, and I'll often say it was at Mommy school. Man, I wish that was something that existed! You can't work in a restaurant without a food handler's card, and you can't drive without training, passing a test, and getting a license, but having a baby? It's like, here's a newborn, good luck! Woah! I think back to myself at 11 when I was babysitting other people's babies. At age 12, my child stands next to me solely in a pair of underwear this morning, complaining about how cold he is and how he needs me to turn on the heater because he doesn't know how to. How about some socks and pants? While we're at it, let's just go all in and add a shirt; why don't we? And then, turn the knob on the nest so it bumps the heater on. I was on a FaceTime call with a dear friend when this happened, and I commented on how he could be so brilliant and yet so clueless at the same time. We laughed so hard when we both said boys simultaneously and then corrected and said, "men" while shaking our heads.

Mama was not my first name, but it will forever be my favorite. And it beats the hell out of Bruh (insert eye roll here). I was that first-time mom that many of us are. You know, the kind of mother who thinks everyone needs hand sanitizer to touch the baby! I damn near killed myself to produce and pump every ounce of breastmilk I could to not fail as a mom because, as we all know, "breast is best," and we only do organic foods. This is as organic as it gets! I just wanted to ensure I did my best for my baby. It's a massive responsibility that I have chosen to take on. So, it's only right that I give it my all, even if it's sometimes messy and I didn't go to Mommy school.

So, for those of you who have been wondering about the title of this book, it's AJ's fault.

As Sophia from The Golden Girls would say, "Picture this," it's 8 pm on a Friday. AJ is 10yrs old at the time. We're sitting on the couch after I picked him up from swim practice. He's in his "jammers," aka spandex long shorts, watching something on his iPad, and as per most of my evenings, I'm working away on my laptop. I see out of the corner of my eye that he has pulled his elastic waistband down so that his privates are hanging out uncovered. In my mind, I'm thinking, "*What in the actual fuck is this boy doing,*" but I pick my battles and instead calmly say, "*AJ, you need to put your privates away.*" In typical defiant AJ fashion, he replies, "*Why?*" I calmly say, "*Because we don't sit in the living room with our privates hanging out.*" He doubles down, asking, "*Why not?*" I try again, calmly restating the obvious. He replies he's "*airing it out.*" (Kids say the darndest things) Again, I attempted to reason with him and stated that he is welcome to air it out in his bedroom or even the thinking room (I'll explain later) but that he can't sit next to me on the couch airing out his junk. Then I get the "*why*" again. He's at that age. So, I go full-on anatomical nurse mode and say, "*Okay, AJ, Mama is gonna take off her pants and underwear and air out my vagina, and you can sit there and air out your penis, and we'll just have an evening of genitals hanging out, okay?*" He quickly tucked that shit back in. Mission accomplished. I took the win. I can't remember ever doing that kind of shit as a little girl? Boys are just a different breed. Seriously.

What's funny is that when I 1st shared with him about my book and its title, he desperately tried to talk me out of it. His concern was voiced as *"Mama, how am I supposed to take your book to school? My teacher is going to be like AJ! What in the world are you reading?! And I'm gonna have to say my mom's book about her vagina?"* My response? Then don't take it to school! Mother of the Year award right here!! Lucky for me, he's come around and even helped me pick the picture for the cover!

The thinking room came about when AJ was two years old. He'd pitch a fit or really get upset, often with him on the floor looking up at his dad screaming, "Why?" and his father towering over him, screaming back, *"Because I said so."* I remember telling his father that someone had to be the adult in the situation, and only one of the two of them was fuckin two years old. I'd tell AJ to go to the sitting room, which is like the formal living room and is rarely used, to "think about his behavior." He started declaring he was going to the thinking room to calm down when upset; we've called it that since. He's now 12 years old, and with his ADHD, dyslexia, and obsessive need for defiance, suffice it to say that he still spends a decent amount of time in the thinking room on a semi-regular basis. As a mom, I use humor and ridiculousness on my part as a way to shock him out of a mood or prevent escalation of frustration regularly. One of the best examples of this he still talks about was at a restaurant a few years back. AJ, myself, and a few other adults were at dinner in a nice restaurant. He was over it, frustrated, and wanted to go. I warned him twice that he needed to be polite and patient and that we'd leave in a bit. I told him if he continued, I'd stand up and dance. AJ can't stand to be embarrassed or have anyone look at him, while lucky for me, I couldn't care less. He incorrectly thought I'd cave and we'd leave, so he continued. I stood in the middle of the restaurant and did my best "cringe dance," as AJ called it. Like Elaine from Seinfeld with the thumbs up and out and all! It was epic; he just about died of embarrassment, but we made it through dinner and have laughed about it ever since!

Boys generally don't appreciate their moms setting boundaries, holding them to high standards, and telling them "NO." AJ hates it with a passion. I hope that when the structure and boundaries help him grow up to be a good human and a man of character who can stand on his own two feet and earn others' respect, he'll thank me for it. Or, at the very least, no longer hate me for it. He pushes me to the brink of insanity on a regular basis. Always challenging me. Always testing just how far he can push me. Holding him accountable and teaching him the lessons of life causes this mama so much frustration, anger, and, most hurtfully, heartache. One of the toughest examples came just before his 12th birthday. He would be with his dad for his birthday and Thanksgiving that year, as they were only days apart and fell around his weekend. With his dad working in the oil field since our divorce, I'd gotten spoiled at having AJ home with me most holidays. I'd planned a birthday dinner for him at a steakhouse where he loves their hamburgers, if you can call meat, cheese, and bread a hamburger (boys!). I had a special cake made of his favorite Naruto anime character, including a picture of him dressed as Kakashi for Halloween. I'd invited my auntie "Coffee" (AJ's great aunt), as AJ calls her, because he couldn't say "Kathy" as a toddler and it stuck. So now she's Aunty Coffee, not to be confused with Anti-Coffee, because we couldn't have that around. Also included were my folks, his Mimi and Papa, and my brother, his uncle. I'd told him we would be in a big hurry when I picked him up after school because we had to run to get the cake and make it to the restaurant to meet everyone at 5 pm. My father was really struggling with heartburn from the radiation treatments for his lung cancer at that time, so the earlier, the better.

I arrived at 15:50, and there was no AJ. I wait until 16:15 and text his friend in chess club with him, asking if they're still practicing (AJ doesn't have a phone because he'd lose his head if it weren't physically attached to his body.) He responds that chess was canceled today. Since school gets out at 15:00 and they apparently didn't have chess, my mama heart really starts pounding. Now it's 16:30, and no AJ. I'm walking the school grounds, knocking on the door of the now completely locked up school, and nothing. At 16:40, I'm in full-on panic mode, and I don't panic! Where is my kid?? I go back up to the main doors and am close to pounding on them when a teacher opens the door to leave. She says the school and the office are closed, and I tell her I cannot find my son. She points to the side just inside the doors and asks if he's one of these two. I lean through the entryway, and AJ and a friend are playing on their laptops. I was so relieved and said, "Yes, ma'am. That one belongs to me."

I told AJ that I'd been waiting for him for over an hour, the school had been out for nearly two, and I was scared to death, to which my demon-spawned son (but with a heart of gold and often quite sensitive and sweet) responded, "*sucks to be you.*" His friend's eyes just about popped out of his head when I said, "*Excuse me? Let's go!*" I turn to walk back to the car, reminding myself that orange is not my color and that if I do what I want to do at this moment, I'll go to jail. I walk back to my truck only to get in and realize AJ isn't following me. I watch in utter disbelief as his friend's brother goes and knocks on the window near where he and his friend are sitting, and I see his friend come running out after immediately grabbing all his things to run after his brother because their mom is waiting. AJ? Nope. Another couple minutes pass, and he comes sauntering out without a care in the world and walks across the school grounds so slowly that a sedated sloth would be faster. He gets in the car and says, "*Hey, mama*" without a care in the world. I had steam blowing out of my ears and thought I might kill him at that moment. Or at least leave him in the school parking lot after telling him to call the mommy store to order a new one.

It absolutely broke this mama's heart, but I called my family, apologizing for the inconvenience and late notice but stating that I'd had an incident with AJ after school and that birthday dinner with cake and their gifts was canceled. I just could not reward such unbelievable disrespect with a birthday dinner at his restaurant of choice with cake and gifts. At that point, AJ said he was sorry and started crying, but I told him he was not, in fact, sorry. He wasn't sorry for what he'd done or for disrespecting me so blatantly. He wasn't sorry that I'd been close to total panic because I couldn't find him. He was sorry because I was holding him accountable, and there were consequences to his behavior. We went on to pick up the special cake I'd had made and went home. I knew it was the right thing to do in my quest to raise a good human, but it just killed me knowing I wouldn't see him on his birthday either. I cried in the shower that night, and I cried about it again the next week when I called to wish him a happy birthday at his dad's. He was at that same restaurant celebrating his birthday with his dad and that side of the family. Sometimes being a good mom is really hard. Like screaming in your car, crying in the shower, and wondering why your neck hurts 24/7 fucking hard!

I have battled my weight my entire life, and I know I will until the day I die. But when AJ was five years old, I weighed in at my all-time high of 348 pounds. I was playing with him in my backyard, and my knees hurt; I was short of breath, and I realized then that if I didn't take action and make a change, I wouldn't be here to raise him. I wasn't going to fulfill my #1 purpose and goal in this life: to raise a good human! I started really changing my diet and took advantage of an otherwise necessary surgical intervention to assist. I'd be damned if I was going to let food and fat win over the love I have for my son. It's now eight years later, and I'm 140 pounds lighter and more comfortable in my own skin than ever. Some people like to diss those who opt for surgical intervention to help them get their health back. You know what? There are many tools available today, and you need to utilize whatever tools you need to get where you want to go. We need to stop judging one another and projecting all this hatred and jealousy. Kindness doesn't cost a thing. Being supportive of someone who's trying their hardest is the mark of a good human being. And how about minding your own fucking business?

AJ is a brilliant, witty, adult-like/dark-humored, and handsome young man. He has a heart of gold and cares deeply for those he loves. Sometimes to a fault. He'll sometimes even shove his own feelings down to spare the feelings of others—something I'm still unlearning at age 45 and doing my best to help him unlearn as well.

Because he struggles with ADHD and Dyslexia, along with the stress of so many changes regarding our divorce a few years ago and him having this "new family" at his dads, his Papa's illness, his worries about his Mama being "alone," changing schools, family drama and estrangement etc., he has at times struggled terribly with poor self-perception and self-worth along with an insatiable desire for love and acceptance. I guess that's all any of us want in life, right? My heart breaks when he displays these struggles. I want him to realize just how beautiful and talented he really is. When he says things like I don't have any friends or no one likes me, it is just heart-wrenching. There was a time there where he would often comment about how stupid he was, and it just killed me because he's actually brilliant, but his struggles with reading and spelling early on made him incredibly critical of himself. One of the things I enjoy the most about my mini-me is his wit and incredible sense of humor. When he feels down and talks about how stupid he is, I often counter by telling him that wit, sarcasm, and stupidity do not go together. You cannot be stupid and super witty with incredible comedic timing. It just doesn't work that way.

I shared with his 3rd-grade teacher while in tears that studying so hard for his spelling tests and still failing miserably was taking a toll on AJ and me. Everyone is a genius. But if you judge a fish by its ability to climb a tree, it will live its whole life believing it's stupid. I am eternally grateful that she pulled me aside and told me that spell check and dictation devices would solve everything. That he had a heart of gold and a brilliant mind that many others would envy.

We were looking at grades a while back, and he had an F in Spanish. He looked at me seriously and said, "I'm dyslexic and having enough trouble with English. You want me to be terrible at another language, too?" He's not wrong.

One of my biggest struggles has been understanding the anger AJ directs at me post-divorce. I'd really like to understand why anything that goes wrong or is not to his liking in his life is somehow my fault. The divorce…my fault. Private to public school…my fault. Putting him in counseling…my fault. Dyslexia tutoring…my fault. Attempting to get him to talk about what's bothering him…my fault. Making him join a sport…my fault. My family dynamics…my fault. Covid as a hospital CEO…my fault. Hell, telling him he smells like butt and must take a bath, and it's my fault. Well, I guess technically telling him he smells like butt is my fault, but seriously? Kids can be such angry little beings, and it's all your fault, of course. Were we like that?

I remember both his counselor and mine saying this is because I'm his safe place. He isn't scared I'm going to leave him. He feels confident in my love and support. It really helped me to read this, and I wanted to share it with all of you!

This is why children are 800% worse when their mother is around:

- Because YOU, mama, are their safe place.

- YOU are the place they can come to with all their problems. If you can't make something better, well, then who can?

- YOU, dear mama, are a garbage disposal for their unpleasant feelings and emotions.

- If a child has been holding it all together all day at school, all weekend at dad's house, or in any other unpleasant situation, the second they see you, they know they can finally let go.

- And BOOM! Does he ever? The "I hate you." The "You're so mean." The "I want to go home" that pierces your heart.

Thankfully, this has calmed down as more time has passed. There aren't the massive swings in his behavior when he goes back and forth between our home and his father's. He has stopped answering with "what happens at daddy's stays at daddy's" when I ask how his visit was. I remember one time I asked him if his step brother was feeling better after having been sick and I was nearly beheaded. He responded that he was his roommate, not his stepbrother!

To all the mamas out there, just know that you're kind of a big deal in your child's eyes, even if they don't always make you feel like it. And in the end, this is a good thing.

AJ's Cigar Box:

I started writing a short letter to AJ each year on his first birthday. When he was really little, it was things like what he learned that year: crawling, walking, first words, etc. This grew to things we'd experienced together or special events that occurred. I include money according to his years of age, so when he was one, it was $10; when he was two, it was $20. My goal is to have something tangible for him to read and look back on and a little cash when I hand it over to him someday, or if, God forbid, something were to happen to me.

I can't always protect him as much as I'd want to. Watching him struggle with bullying and finding out that he'd begun to weigh himself and count calories at age nine was horrifying to me. Mostly because I've been there and done that. I chose bulimia rather than anorexia for years. I didn't share that piece with AJ yet, but I do often remind him that it took me nine months to form that heart he has in his chest, and I'll be damned if somebody else is going to break it with cruel words in a matter of seconds.

Kids can be incredibly cruel to one another. I think it's partly because their brains are literally not fully developed yet, so they don't have the emotional or intellectual capacity to properly understand and/or regulate themselves. Heck, I know very few adults who are that mature or self-aware. However, I do feel like, as parents, we need to do better. Yes, it's a tough job, but it's a responsibility we've chosen to take on for the rest of our lives, and we owe it to our children to teach them how to be kind, caring, aware, contributing citizens of this global village we are all a part of.

On that note, AJ and I started traveling together intentionally solo at least once a year several years back. We call it our mama/AJ trip and AJ is in charge of selecting the destination annually. This tradition started at AJ's request as we were returning from a trip to Florida with my folks to visit my sister just after my divorce. We did Halloween at Disney, with the two of us dressed as Toothless and Light Fury, and his Mimi in her best Minnie Mouse outfit. So much fun with my sister and niece. AJ learned to do the floss dance while waiting in line thanks to his Uncle Scott and ran backwards with his cousin Avery to his heart's content through the parks. However, as we prepared to land back in El Paso he said "Mama. Can we please go on a trip with just you and me sometime?" I told him absolutely IF he promised that we would continue to do so when he was older, and I wasn't cool anymore even if for just a weekend annually. He thought about it and then put his pinky up and said "Deal! Let's pinky promise!" That has been our thing forever on important things. We pinky promise.

As life, or Murphy's law would have it, we have had to reschedule a few of these, but they are a priority of mine to this day. We had to postpone the 1st annual Mama/AJ trip because of a little thing called a global pandemic. However, the Ninjago room at Legoland California and SeaWorld San Diego were waiting for us when the world finally reopened. Another time we had to scramble and reroute from Yellowstone when it flooded and closed a week prior to our trip. But Sedona, the Grand Canyon, and Antelope Canyon with a side trip to slide rock filled in just fine. These annual trips have become something we both look forward to and fulfills my goal of collecting memories and experiences with AJ, instead of just stuff!

As much of a little asshole as he can be at times, he's my asshole, and I love him more than life itself. I will until the day I die. My snuggle-butt, munchkalinos, shmo, snugs, stinkapodamous, pita, and most importantly, my precious AJ.

YOU are this mama's why.

Chapter 23

Allie 2.0

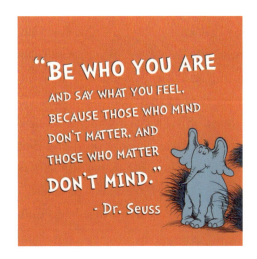

This book is the start of Allie 2.0. Actually, it's already started. I've learned so much about myself and life going through this process. It's been a wild ride; I'll tell you that much. After lots of tears, many belly laughs, and some trepidation about what to share and withhold (for the sake of other people), I find myself writing the final chapter of my first book. Not the final chapter of my life, as I feel like that's just getting started in many ways! When they say it's hard to write a book, they're not kidding. I have a newfound respect for people who do this for a living. It's also helped me take stock of what I'm currently doing with my life and where I see myself in years to come. We only get to live life once, so why aren't we running like we're on fire toward our wildest dreams?

Maybe part of Allie 2.0 is the idea that at some point, we have to say, "Fuck this shit," and rise to become all we are meant to be. We have to kick ass and take names even when it's hard because you never know when it might be your last opportunity to do so. And that's a scary thought. It's what makes life so valuable. The fact that it can come to an end at any moment.

Ever heard someone say, "Fuck around and find out?" Well, that's exactly where I'm at in my life, and I plan on doing just that! Perhaps I'll fuck around and stop giving a shit about other people's opinions of my life. Maybe I'll fuck around and finally kick my co-dependent tendencies that have me staying in relationships and tolerating family dynamics I shouldn't. Fuck around and achieve my bucket list goal of writing a book and running my own business. Fuck around and find myself living my dream of encouraging others through my life experiences via podcast appearances, public speaking engagements, or even a TED talk. Why the hell not? Maybe, just maybe, I'll fuck around and find even more of ME in the process!

We tend to sit around and worry about all kinds of stuff we have no control over. Other people's opinions, how others perceive us, what others think we should do, potential failure, not getting it right, screwing up, world events, etc. The only thing you can control in your life is YOU! The thoughts you allow yourself to focus on, what you put in your body, the emotions you allow yourself to hold onto, whether you move your body or not, the behavior you allow yourself to engage in, and how and to what level you choose *to allow* others to impact your life and wellbeing. You can't control other people. So stop trying. Focus on what's most important. YOURSELF! Learn to say yes, but more importantly, how to say no! No to disrespect, no to anything that's below your standards, no to people who are just in your life to see how much they can get from you, no to half-assing anything in life, no to anything that does not fit in with your vision or is not in alignment with your greatest purpose.

"Daring to set boundaries is about having the courage to love ourselves even when we risk disappointing others." — Brené Brown

I've started and stopped the process of writing this completely honest and unbelievably vulnerable book many times out of fear. Fear of hurting someone's feelings with my honesty. Fear of getting fired for speaking the truth. Fear of what other people will think of how I am living my life. Fear of…..

Instead, I've chosen to move past that fear and flip the narrative on its head. I'm not afraid, I'm EXCITED!!! I've requested different people to provide sustenance and cover different bills should the ax come down. You all know who you are and what you're responsible for covering! I've explained to AJ we may be eating an awful lot of Cup a' Noodles here for a bit if that happens, but LOVED his response when he said "but we'll be eating it together mama!" I was talking to Royal Flush about being scared of how those addressed in the book may react. He said something pretty powerful and very impactful to me which was "Did you lie about anyone? Is your intent to hurt anyone? Because if not, then who cares!" I also shared my fears with Greece, who encouraged me as well by saying that the truth is not punishable. He's on the hook for my coffee should things go sideways! My goal here was to stand in my power and share my story. Period. And that is exactly what I have done.

All of this sounds so easy, but trust me when I say I FULLY understand that it is anything but. I was so worried about blowing up relationships, friendships, and even family when I started out on this journey. I held off for so long, changed paths, paused projects, and even talked myself out of it once or twice. When I started doing the work to identify who I am and what I want for my life, some people fell by the wayside, naturally.

Others became more important than ever. One or two threw tantrums related to my newfound self-respect and boundaries, losing me forever. That is some painful shit I wouldn't wish upon anyone, my worst enemy included. However, the respect I gained for myself, the self-love, the appreciation I found for who I am at my core, along with the realization that if I don't pick myself, stand up for myself, respect myself, and have my own back, I can be sure as shit no one else will. It has been absolutely worth it. The losses were hard. Ugly crying, snot running, screaming in a pillow, fucking hard. In some ways, it's like I saw the light and can't unsee it. I can't go back to head in the sand, fake it til you make it, and if it looks good, it is good. Now I ask questions like: "Does it fill my cup or add to my life somehow?" Have I told you on multiple occasions that when you do "x," it really bothers me or hurts me or makes me feel a certain way, yet you just keep doing it? Or not doing it, depending on the situation. If so, I'm out! A friend recently sent me a meme, and it was hella funny but spot on. If it doesn't bring me joy, money, laughter, or orgasms, I'm a hard no!

But on the other side of the horrific moments of realizing the losses coming from my growth, I have no regrets. There are some fracture lines in my heart, yeah, without a doubt. But I have zero regrets. I have always been real. Raw. Authentic. Same Allie in the boardroom as in the bar, remember? What I hadn't always done was be honest with myself about what was best for me. I spent so many years ensuring everyone else was comfortable and happy and rescued that I lost myself. It's been a lot. It's been heavy and hard, but I'm so grateful for the journey and all I've learned and continue to. And guess what? I found ME through this process. Who I am at my core. What I want for myself. What makes ME happy, and what makes ME sad. What I like and don't like. And I realized that it is the right of every single one of us to choose what we will and will not tolerate in our lives. Yes, even from friends and family. The idea that blood is thicker than water and we don't get to pick our family? Agree to disagree. Someone well-intentioned, I'm sure, said to me when I made a difficult decision about a family member that they never had that luxury. I said it wasn't a luxury. It was life or death. I reminded them of the old adage they'd always shared with me about the fence and anger. The father teaches his son to hammer nails into the fence when he's angry and then pull them out when he's not. Noting that the hole left by that nail represents the idea that the damage done by our words or actions in the heat of the moment causes irreparable harm to others. I said, while sobbing with snot running down my face, that if I were that fence, there's no fucking fence left. Just a giant gaping hole where Allie used to be. I had to pick myself to ensure I was still here to finish raising my why! The scariest thing to realize is that what we tolerate becomes the standard for what we receive. Try that one on for size!

"What you permit, you promote. What you allow, you encourage. What you condone, you own." - Unknown

I recall a time in my mid-30s when I voiced actually being afraid of being too happy because I was waiting for the other shoe to drop. The idea that something tragic would happen soon and wreck it all. I vividly remember talking to a long-time team member turned dear friend, saying that I was married to my best friend, we had a healthy, happy baby boy, and my career was taking off. I said I felt so blessed and grateful but somehow also felt unworthy. It turns out that it is far more common than I realized in people who experience anxiety, or what's called anticipatory anxiety. It's also common in people who have experienced a great deal of adverse experiences in childhood or those who have lived through trauma. Your nervous system was once put into a state of feeling extremely unsafe, so now it's constantly waiting for it to happen again. Constantly looking out for a sign of any potential danger or disappointment. I've committed myself to finding moments of joy in my days and to the concept that if there are tons of them for a bit, I will enjoy every minute of it. I've recognized that EVERYTHING ends eventually. The good luck streak. The bad luck streak. The blessings. The curses. The joy. The pain. So, I choose to enjoy the joy, cherish the glimmers, and hold on for dear life during the difficulties that are certain to follow.

I've made it through 100% of my challenges alive thus far, and so have you.

I plan to put myself first and not fucking apologize for it anymore! Realistically, maybe second when needed when it comes to AJ, but STILL noteworthy because I'm no longer putting myself last. That's progress!

In Grey's Anatomy, there's a scene where Meredith says to McDreamy, *"Pick me. Choose me. Love me."* Well, I pick me! I choose me! And from now on, I will love myself! Allie in my entirety. Not just Allie as a sister, daughter, mother, niece, co-worker, boss, friend, etc. I am permitting myself to just be ME!

This comeback is personal! It's my apology to myself for putting up with shit I didn't deserve for so many years.

Do you know what it takes for a star to shine? A shitload of fucking darkness! No one warns you about the amount of grieving you have to go through while on this journey of personal growth. The pain in realizing that the people you thought would be part of your life forever are actually only supposed to be there for a season and letting go of the picture in your mind of how things are supposed to be can be extremely challenging. The hurt that comes with setting boundaries and enforcing them when the people you love try to cross them is soul-crushing. Because you were never taught how to and never had the self-worth to teach yourself. Well, I now have the self-worth I have always been searching for and have finally given myself permission to stand up for myself. It's taken a long time, but here the fuck I am. I've found that when you've truly leveled up, you begin to recognize patterns, and things that don't fill your cup start to look a lot more like, "No, thank you," and, "Fuck this shit!" No, it's not easy, but it's also extremely liberating just to allow yourself to exist the way you've always wanted to. And it's a process. It doesn't just happen overnight. Look at me. I'm halfway into my fourth decade on this planet, and it's taken me this long to learn that it's okay to just be myself and that it's okay to allow myself to say no.

It's time you unlearned the things you learned from wounded people or what was imposed onto you while surviving your own traumas. It's time to heal and move on. It's time to *let go* and *let them.* Hurt people, hurt people. But that doesn't make it okay. I choose the opposite path, where healed people go on to help others on their own healing journeys. The work works!

Do you know what most people regret in their old age or on their deathbed? Not having taken more chances. Not having gone after their dreams, having allowed themselves to hold themselves back because of the fear of failure or the opinions of others. Not writing the book. Not taking the trip. Not eating the cake. Not quitting the toxic job. Not starting the business they wanted to launch. Don't make the same mistakes. You have an opportunity here—a choice to make. Pick you. Choose you. Love you!

Adele…stunningly beautiful. Incredibly talented. Refreshingly real. And part of the A-Team, if I may point out (amazing people whose names start with A), I've been told a handful of times by a few different people that I remind them of her, and I always respond with "I wish." Yes, because she's drop-dead gorgeous and can sing better than just about anyone I've ever heard, but for me, it is more her person. Her choice to live authentically. To be her hilariously funny, sarcastically witty, f-bomb-dropping, unapologetic self. To own her shit and to choose herself and her son above all else.

After her big comeback debut with the Oprah interview and private concert on the world stage, so many haters criticized her decision to delay her concerts. Not I! In fact, I thought even more highly of her for just being real! For her strength to simply say no when all eyes were on her. Despite all the pressure and all the expectations, Adele had the strength to do what was best for her! She wasn't quite ready for the full-on launch of Adele 2.0 yet! And not only did she have the chesticles to say so, but look at her now!

I had the extraordinary opportunity to see her in all her glory at her residency in Vegas. Thank you, Royal Flush!! Seeing her live had been on my bucket list since I saw her perform Rolling in the Deep on Dancing with the Stars in 2012. I vividly remember thinking she was amazing and vowing to see her one day. I came close over a year ago, but life circumstances shifted a bit, and I thought, well, there went that, so to have another chance was magic, and I took it! And it was meant to be! I was there for her 70th show, which she shared during the concert. It was also the two-year anniversary of what was supposed to have been her Vegas residency launch. My eyes welled up immediately when she shared that because that single decision is what I admire most and what made her a queen in my eyes!

Imagine if we all found a way to make the tough decisions with ourselves and our wellbeing at the forefront. To choose what's right rather than just what's easy or accepted. Not what the boss, partner, family member, or peer pressure and society says you need to do, but rather what YOU need to do for YOU! #gamechanger. So, to say I want to be Adele when I grow up might be an understatement and also impossible because she's far younger than I.

Sometimes, we have to forget what we feel and remember what we deserve. And take nothing less! You will always be miserable if you allow your emotions to dictate your life. Learn how to regulate your thoughts and your emotions. There are tons of resources out there for you to learn from on the topic. Start to empower yourself with tools and strategies so you can live your best life without making yourself small so others will feel more comfortable. Fuck other people. (Not literally. Well, unless they're good at it. Life's also too short for bad sex.) Are they going to live your dreams for you? No. Are they going to pay your bills? No. Then, who the hell cares what they think or have to say?

I'm creating the woman I want to be, so please excuse me while I become far more protective of myself, my time, and my energy. I don't have time for assholes anymore. I no longer have time for wicked intentions, lukewarm sentiments, or pettiness. Fake? Forget it! When someone asks me if I have someone special in my life, I've learned to say, "Yes." Me! I think I'm the one I've been looking for.

"Change is hard at first, messy in the middle, and gorgeous in the end."
- Robin Sharma

Even though many things, people, and instances have broken my heart, they've also fixed my vision. I'm grateful for that. I'm grateful for my mistakes, hardships, and challenges. Each of them presents me with an opportunity to learn and grow as a person. My biggest fear is no longer failing. I celebrate every opportunity I get to live my life how I want. I celebrate the fact that I have the capacity and ability to learn from the experiences I have in this life.

I have accepted that it is okay to be an incredibly strong, goal-oriented, self-sufficient as fuck woman, but still want to be swept off of my feet, loved, appreciated, and cared for by the right partner. I want to be clear here. I've said in places in this book that we don't need men. That does NOT mean I don't WANT that wonderful man in my life. That I don't WANT a partner in every sense of the word. That we don't WANT that protective, providing, masculine energy in our lives. I simply mean that in today's society, we can navigate the world without it AND be happy. BUT the right man as a partner, YES, PLEASE!

You don't have to choose one over the other. I want it all! Anything short of everything is just not worth accepting, as I have so much to offer. I no longer dim my light for anyone. If it bothers them, they can wear a pair of sunglasses. It's not my problem.

I saw and shared a meme just yesterday that said, "in this season of my life, I'm choosing people who choose me, prioritize people who prioritize our connection, and making intentional space for reciprocal relationships rooted in clarity and care". I couldn't have said it better myself! One-sided, one-way relationships are in my rearview mirror regardless of where they originated.

I don't want to "go to work" anymore. I want to "go to my passion." I won't be a slave to the golden handcuffs. I want to make as much of a difference to as many people as possible for as long as I get to exist on this planet. I want to get up in the morning feeling excited about the day ahead because I know I get to do what I love. The most wonderful moment in a woman's life is when she realizes that she can do what she wants, when she wants, how she wants, and she doesn't owe anyone an explanation. She doesn't need anyone's permission. She's just living her life. And it's beautiful.

For me, the realization that certain people in my life saw me as a competition rather than the friend or family member I thought I was to them was heartbreaking. I've just been going about the day-to-day of life while trying to be my best self, trying to learn more about myself, and continuing to grow and improve as a mom, a friend, a boss, a co-worker, and a family member. I don't care to compete with anyone but me. It took me a while to accept the painful fact that we cannot control other people's perceptions of us. We have no say in how our actions or success makes someone else feel. I do think the brighter your light and the higher you climb, the more people perceive you as someone with power and privilege. The more successful or powerful someone perceives you to be, the more quiet haters or outright attackers you will attract. I had to learn that their perceptions are theirs alone. I can't change them and have stopped trying. Ultimately, I choose to continue living my life on my terms. I am a kind and supportive person who loves to see the success of those around me. It's exciting and thrilling to see someone else succeed in life. But I also learned to feel comfortable and empowered to remove people who blatantly disregard my feelings or my well-being in an attempt to change me or to change others' perceptions of me. People will believe what they choose to believe, and other people's opinions of me are none of my business. So why pay any attention to it?

It's our ability to love and be loved that makes us human. By today's standards, perhaps it's more accurate to say that our ability to select each image that contains stairs or a stop light accurately makes us human.

Jokes aside. I think technology is awesome, but it has also played a significant role in how disconnected we've become as a species. I really feel like we need to get back to investing in our communities. Remember that we're all human beings. We all have red blood running through our veins. Well, everyone except me, as we've already established that my veins are full of coffee. We all have challenges we face on a daily basis that no one else knows about. How about we just start being more kind, understanding, caring, supportive, and loving towards one another? Really, what does it take away from you to cheer someone else on? Nothing. What does it cost to be kind to someone else? Nothing. What does it take to be a caring human being? Not much. But we're constantly spending more and more time judging and criticizing content creators all over the internet, saying mean things we'd never say to someone's face just because of the false security anonymity gives us. It's bullshit! Who cares what kind of potato you are, according to some quiz on social media? Go volunteer in your community and help make someone's life just a little bit better, you asshat.

Just a funny, the word volunteer made me think of real quick...A friend of mine is the executive director for a non-profit organization with an incredibly important mission to support victims of human trafficking and educate the public on the topic. Imagine my horror when AJ said to a group of people "oh yeah. That's Nic. My mama's friend that runs the human trafficking business"! I wanted to crawl under the table, but luckily my tribe, Nic included, all died laughing at the misnomer. I will say she is most definitely doing her part to make this world a better place! You go girl!!

For now, I'm praying for the woman I'll be in five years' time. I hope she's happy, healthy, and loved, living life unapologetically and doing what she loves. In the meantime, I'm choosing to be strong, resilient, and unapologetically me. I choose to invest my time, money, and energy into my personal growth and into those who are truly on this journey with me. I choose to become the best version of myself I can possibly be so I can also be the best mama for my son that I can possibly be.

"The hardest and most important decision you can ever make is to choose yourself. It may mean you upset some people in your life. You'll raise eyebrows. You'll be gossiped about. It will be hard. So fucking what? The only thing that you have to lose is the weight of everybody else's opinions. What you have to gain is freedom. Your happiness is more important than anyone else's opinion about it." - Mel Robbins

Nelson Mandela said we cannot be prepared for something while secretly believing it will never happen. I believe that this part of my journey is here to teach me how to be a better version of myself and how to live this gift that is life that has been given to me to the best of my abilities.

Your life is yours to live. It's your responsibility to go after what you want. No one else can or should do it for you. As hard as it may be to hear, no one else is responsible for your happiness, success, health, well-being, or your lack thereof. YOU are the only one responsible for your life. That is unless you're literally unable to do it yourself or you're two years old. It was during a heartbreaking conversation not all that long ago that my mom said to me "do NOT give up on your dreams Catherine Alexander Trimble!" She shared that she had given up on her dreams years ago and didn't want to see me do the same. It broke my heart and I vowed never to do the same. I really hope you'll choose to do whatever it takes to not waste even a second of this life on anything that does not bring you joy, growth, love, or good health.

I choose to take a leap of faith, armed with grit, grace, and gratitude! I hope you do, too.

Conclusion

Well, what a ride it has been. I feel like I've been on the rollercoaster ride of my life while writing this book.

My greatest hope is that you will have found something that made you laugh, something that drew a tear to your eye, something that gave you an aha moment, something that made you feel more motivated, and something new you learned within these pages. Even if it's just one of these, I'll take it.

Like I said from the beginning: if just one woman feels a little less batshit crazy after having read this book, I will have accomplished my mission in airing out my vagina!

I have learned so much up until and throughout this process, and I look forward to what lies ahead for me. I now know I am capable of more than

I ever realized. For the first time, I'm living life on my terms. For the first time ever, I am choosing myself first.

Right now, I'm looking forward to seeing my story continue to unfold. I plan on doing more things that make me feel good about myself. I look forward to pursuing my passions and helping others do the same. My dream is to build my new business as a consultant, helping others by sharing what I've learned in my personal and professional capacities. Perhaps a talk here and there. There's always the dream of standing on the stage at a TED Talk.

I also look forward to watching my boy AJ grow up as he joins me on this journey that is our crazy life. There are still so many adventures to be had. Where to on our next Mama/AJ trip snugs?? It's time to plan!

I look forward to spending the rest of my life becoming the best version of myself and living my very best life. No more surviving for this girl. It's time to live!

Oh, oh, here she comes. Watch out, boy, she'll chew you up.

Sources

[1] Howard, H. (2022, January 17). *Just do it! How murderer Gary Gilmore's final words demanding firing squad officers pull their triggers inspired Nike's famous slogan*. The Daily Mail. Retrieved September 25, 2023, from https://www.dailymail.co.uk/news/article-10411375/Just-murderer-Gary-Gilmores-final-words-inspired-Nikes-famous-slogan.html

[2] The Phrase Finder (n.d.). *The meaning and origin of the expression: Tits-up*. Retrieved September 28, 2023, from https://www.phrases.org.uk/meanings/385050.html

[3] [JAX]. (2023, March 3). *Jax - Cinderella Snapped (Official Lyric Video)* [Video]. YouTube. https://www.youtube.com/watch?v=oRfEqCap1I8

[4] [Kesha]. (2020, July 9). *Bastards* [Video]. YouTube. https://www.youtube.com/watch?v=VfMtTmZ0MPc

[5] [PINK]. (2011, January 19). *Fuckin' Perfect* [Video]. YouTube. https://www.youtube.com/watch?v=ocDlOD1Hw9k

Made in the USA
Columbia, SC
14 October 2024

44365853R00133